Treating the Homeless: Urban Psychiatry's Challenge

Treating the Homeless: Urban Psychiatry's Challenge

Edited by
BILLY E. JONES, M.D.

Director, Department of Psychiatry, Lincoln Medical and Mental Health Center, Bronx, New York; and Professor of Clinical Psychiatry, New York Medical College, Valhalla, New York

AMERICAN PSYCHIATRIC PRESS, INC.
Washington, D.C.

© 1986 American Psychiatric Press, Inc.

Manufactured in the U.S.A.

The paper used in this publication meets the minimum requirements of American National Standard for Information Sciences—Permanence of Papers for Printed Library Materials, ANSI Z39.48-1984.

Library of Congress Cataloging in Publication Data

Main entry under title:

Treating the Homeless.

     (Clinical insights)
     Includes bibliographies.
     1. Homeless persons—Mental health services—United States. 2. Mentally ill—United States. 3. Community mental health services—United States. 4. Chronically ill—Mental health services—United States. I. Jones, Billy E., 1938- . II. Series. [DNLM: 1. Community Mental Health Services. 2. Mental Disorders—therapy. 3. Transients and Migrants. WA 305 T784]
RC451.4.H64T74   1986   362.2'0425   85-30626
ISBN 0-88048-080-7 (soft)

Contents

Contributors

A. ANTHONY ARCE, M.D.

Professor and Deputy Chairman, Department of Mental Health Sciences,
Hahnemann University Hospital, Philadelphia, Pennsylvania

SUSAN BARROW, PH.D.

Research Scientist, Community Support Services Evaluation Unit, New York
State Psychiatric Institute, New York

RODGER K. FARR, M.D.

Chief, Medical and Psychiatric Consultation Services, Los Angeles County
Department of Mental Health, Los Angeles; Founder of the Los Angeles Skid
Row Project; and Assistant Clinical Professor of Psychiatry, University of
Southern California College of Medicine, Los Angeles

DEBORAH B. GOLDSTEIN, PH.D.

Coordinator of Psychiatric Education, Department of Psychiatry, Lincoln
Medical and Mental Health Center, Bronx, New York; and Instructor of
Psychiatry, New York Medical College, Valhalla, New York

KOSTAS GOUNIS, M.A.

Research Scientist, Evaluation Research Unit, New York State Office of Mental
Health, Albany, New York

BEVERLY A. GRAY, M.A.

Coordinator of the Research Unit, Department of Psychiatry, Lincoln Medical
and Mental Health Center, Bronx, New York; and Instructor of Psychiatry,
New York Medical College, Valhalla, New York

BILLY E. JONES, M.D.

Director, Department of Psychiatry, Lincoln Medical and Mental Health
Center, Bronx, New York; and Professor of Clinical Psychiatry, New York
Medical College, Valhalla, New York

STEVEN E. KATZ, M.D.

Commissioner, New York State Office of Mental Health, Albany, New York;
Professor of Clinical Psychiatry, New York University School of Medicine,
New York; and Clinical Professor of Psychiatry, Albany Medical College,
Albany, New York

IRENE SHIFREN LEVINE, PH.D.

Associate Director, Division of Education and Service Systems Liaison, National Institute of Mental Health, Rockville, Maryland

FRANK LIPTON, M.D.

Director, Psychiatric Emergency Services, Bellevue Hospital, New York; and Assistant Clinical Professor of Psychiatry, New York University School of Medicine, New York

PETER MICHEELS, M.A.

Staff Psychologist, Bellevue Psychiatric Hospital, New York; and Clinical Instructor of Psychiatry, New York University Medical Center, New York

JOSEPH P. MORRISSEY, PH.D.

Director, Evaluation Research Unit, New York State Office of Mental Health, Albany, New York

JAMES W. STOCKDILL, M.A.

Director, Division of Education and Service Systems Liaison, National Institute of Mental Health, Rockville, Maryland

ELMER L. STRUENING, PH.D.

Director, Community Support Services Evaluation Unit, New York State Psychiatric Institute, New York

MICHAEL J. VERGARE, M.D.

Associate Chairman, Department of Psychiatry, Albert Einstein Medical Center Northern Division, Philadelphia; and Associate Professor, Department of Psychiatry, Temple University, Philadelphia, Pennsylvania

Introduction

The existence of the homeless in our urban centers is no longer shocking news—it is accepted fact. While the numbers may still be debated, the presence of the homeless is highly visible and well documented. The unkempt women with their bags and the tattered men with their layers of clothing are all around our teeming inner cities. Their plight and needs have become a major problem for society. Food, shelter, warmth, and health care for the homeless must be provided. The delivery of these services is new and requires much thought and planning.

The mentally ill homeless, reported in most studies to be approximately 50 percent of the homeless population, are among this group who need services, especially treatment. Some are the deinstitutionalized chronic mentally ill, while others are the young chronic mentally ill who have had acute hospital stays. Providing mental health treatment to these homeless persons is a new endeavor fraught with many problems. Treating the homeless is psychiatry's newest challenge. It is also undoubtedly one of the most difficult.

There are many issues and problem areas that must be considered and addressed in treating the mentally ill homeless. Some of the issues include the following:

1. The homeless have many pressing needs, and mental health care is not likely to be considered a high priority. "Making it" on the streets or in a shelter in a large city can truly be a task in survival. Mental health services must be an integral part of a network of services that meets basic needs.

2. The homeless are mobile and free to move from place to place. There can be no catchment boundaries or residence and eligibility requirements. A treatment program must be open to admission and discharge based primarily on the desires of the homeless, with the exception of a small number who require involuntary treatment.

3. While estimates of the number of homeless exist, there is no clear documented count or census. This poses another problem for planning treatment services.

4. Services must be accessible to the homeless. This means treatment services must be rendered on the streets and provided in facilities located in the areas where the homeless congregate, as well as in shelters. Mobile crisis and skid row storefront services are needed.

5. Time and structure are not important elements in the lives of the homeless. Hence it may be difficult for them to keep appointments and to comply with structured treatment programs.

These problems involve planning and mental health treatment delivery, but consideration of the modalities and content of mental health treatment for the homeless is equally important. What treatment programs work and what should be the content? This is indeed psychiatry's challenge in treating the homeless. Research studies and innovative, new treatment programs are being conducted. In this monograph, which is based in part on material presented at the 137th Annual Meeting of the American Psychiatric Association, we will report on some of the studies and describe some of the new treatment approaches.

In Chapter 1, Dr. Levine and Mr. Stockdill present a comprehensive review of the plight of the homeless. They examine the extent of the problem and discuss the factors involved in the severely mentally ill becoming and remaining homeless. They report on the private and public policies which have attempted to address the needs of the homeless, particularly the mentally ill homeless. They also discuss the leadership that they believe can be provided by mental health professionals.

In Chapter 2, Drs. Vergare and Arce report on the findings of two studies conducted to investigate mental illness among the homeless. In discussing program development for the homeless, they emphasize the necessity of coordination and collaboration among social, medical, and psychiatric services and agencies. They focus on the importance of providing mental health services in shelters or residential centers for the homeless.

In Chapter 3, Drs. Lipton and Sabatini, and Mr. Micheels, present the results of a study they conducted on 50 homeless men and women. Their results indicate that a number of the subjects suffered from chronic mental illness. They review several factors which should be considered in providing services to the homeless.

In Chapter 4, Dr. Jones, Ms. Gray, and Dr. Goldstein report on a study involving 150 homeless persons who had no history of psychiatric hospitalization. Subjects were interviewed in the streets and shelters of New York City. Self-report measures were administered, and the resulting psychosocial data are presented with a discussion of the relevance of the findings to mental health professionals.

Dr. Farr, in Chapter 5, also focuses on the necessity for a collaborative effort between the public and private sectors in addressing the problems of the mentally ill homeless. His presentation of the Los Angeles Skid Row Project discusses creative and innovative approaches in developing programs to help the mentally ill homeless.

In Chapter 6, Dr. Morrissey and colleagues discuss the development of a shelter for the mentally ill homeless. They present a detailed account of the collaboration between the public and private sectors in providing care for the mentally ill homeless. Their program is innovative and provides examples of what can be done for the homeless.

The chapters in this monograph address both the issues of mental health treatment delivery and content. In addition, the contributors discuss many of the generic problems of the homeless who may experience psychological trauma.

I wish to acknowledge and thank Beverly Gray, M.A., and Deborah Goldstein, Ph.D, for their assistance and help in the preparation of this monograph.

Billy E. Jones, M.D.

1

Mentally Ill and Homeless: A National Problem

Irene Shifren Levine, Ph.D.
James W. Stockdill, M.A.

1

Mentally Ill and Homeless: A National Problem

Many persons across the nation who are seriously mentally ill lack safe and decent shelter (1). In order to remedy this disturbing situation, their advocates are waging a battle on several fronts: at the portals of private emergency shelters that deny entry to the mentally ill; at local hearings where communities are fighting to maintain exclusionary zoning practices; at budget hearings before state and county legislatures and in other arenas where disability groups compete for the paucity of public housing and residential treatment programs; and in the "competitive" housing market where the mentally ill are often denied access to apartments by landlords. The battle has even moved to the courtroom, which has recently affirmed the right of the mentally ill to seek entitlement to shelter and to have the decision rendered by a court of law (2).

As the number and visibility of homeless persons in America have increased and become the focus of growing media and professional concern, mental health advocates have begun to realize that

The opinions expressed in this chapter are those of the authors and do not represent the official position of the National Institute of Mental Health.

This chapter is a substantially revised and updated version of a paper presented by Dr. Levine at the 137th Annual Meeting of the American Psychiatric Association, Los Angeles, California, May 1984.

they must join forces with other professional and lay persons: to more rationally understand the problem of homelessness, to examine its relationship to mental illness and mental health service delivery, and to assure responsibility for its complex resolution. This chapter attempts to review the scope of what the mental health community and others have done to address the problems of those who are mentally ill and homeless.

SCOPE AND EXTENT OF THE PROBLEM OF HOMELESSNESS NATIONALLY

Because the homeless are often a population without addresses, without records, and lacking in community ties, one can only make informed guesses about their numbers. The two most frequently cited estimates of the number of homeless persons in America, which create a nominal range, are 250,000 and 2.2 million persons. The first figure (250,000) represents the lowest estimated *daily* count of homeless persons used by the Department of Housing and Urban Development (DHUD) in its controversial May 1, 1984, national report on the problem of homelessness (3). If one uses this number and takes into account the large turnover among the homeless, the cumulative annual count could range well between two or three times the daily total (4). The second figure (2.2 million) was reported in 1982 by the Washington-based Center for Creative Non-Violence, an advocacy group for the homeless; it represents an annual estimate derived by assuming that approximately one percent of the population lacks shelter (5). Neither of these estimates is based on a systematic study or actual count of the universe of homeless persons in America. Moreover, the wide discrepancy between the numbers suggests the extent of the methodological and political problems that arise in attempting to define, locate, and count the homeless population.

In a recent report on homelessness, the United States General Accounting Office noted that the problem has increased in recent years "although there are no reliable data to identify how much it is increasing" (6). We also know that although homelessness is not a new phenomenon, the profile of the "typical" homeless person has changed considerably from the time when the homeless were confined to the skid row areas of our cities. The ranks of the middle-aged, white, single alcoholic male have recently been swelled by the addition of younger people, families, minorities, and children—and by the addition of a large and growing subgroup of persons who have serious and persistent mental disorders, the severely mentally ill. Although there are differences among geographic areas, several patterns have emerged (5):

1. The average age of the homeless person is in the mid-thirties, much younger than in the past;

2. Approximately 15–25 percent of the homeless are women, a percentage that seems to be increasing;

3. Approximately 40–50 percent of the homeless are minorities, a percentage that is also increasing (with the racial and ethnic composition dependent on the specific local area);

4. Between 20 and 30 percent of the homeless are in family groups, which include children; and

5. One-half to two-thirds of the homeless have completed high school, and approximately 25–30 percent have attended college.

MENTAL ILLNESS AMONG THE HOMELESS

Although we have no uniform national data on the homeless, a growing number of disparate state and local studies have found that a significant proportion of the homeless suffer from serious mental illness. One of the largest of these studies was funded by by the National Institute of Mental Health (NIMH) in Ohio (7). In a sample of nearly 1,000 persons in 32 counties, almost one-third of those surveyed (30.8 percent) were found to have current psychiatric problems requiring some form of mental health service. Eighteen percent of the sample had experienced at least one psychiatric hospitalization in a state hospital.

Three national reports have focused on the proportion of mentally ill among the homeless:

1. The recently published report of the American Psychiatric Association's Task Force on the Homeless Mentally Ill noted that "in most universes of homeless people, between 25 and 50 percent have serious and chronic forms of mental illness" (8).

2. An August 1984 analysis of the problems of the homeless, prepared for the President by the Department of Health and Human Services (DHHS), suggested that "from 33 to 66 percent of the homeless in shelters are characterized principally by mental illness, on an acute or chronic basis," and that "25–35 percent are former patients of mental hospitals" (5).

3. The report to the Secretary of HUD, mentioned earlier, noted that 22 percent of the shelter population is mentally ill and that the national survey probably "understates the incidence of mental illness" (3).

Obviously, one can anticipate differences in the prevalence of mental illness in different geographic samples, in shelter-based versus street populations, and in urban versus rural populations. For some who are homeless, mental illness is a contributing cause to their homelessness; for others, emotional distress is a consequence of their homelessness. Since we are in an era of deinstitutionalization, we can expect that some of those who are severely mentally ill will have histories of hospitalization and that others will not. Different sampling techniques may even yield different findings in the same locale when studies are conducted by different investigators under different institutional auspices. However, despite differences in overall numbers, there is relative agreement that the severely mentally ill comprise a significant proportion of the homeless.

FACTORS IN THE SEVERELY MENTALLY ILL BECOMING OR REMAINING HOMELESS

A number of societal or contextual factors have contributed to the problem of homelessness in America. They include: urban renewal and the lack of low-cost housing; unemployment; the complexity and discontinuity of our social service system; and the disintegration of the nuclear family. Each of these factors also contributes to homelessness among the mentally ill who, because of their disability, are generally at the bottom rung of the socioeconomic ladder. Obtaining affordable housing is a particularly difficult problem for the mentally ill person, who often has a limited income (1). Historically, "rooming" houses have provided a lower-priced housing alternative for those who could not afford larger apartments. Five years ago, there were 53,000 single-room occupancy units in New York City; now there are 15,000 (5). Boston has lost 75 percent of its low income housing in the last ten years (D. Mauch, personal communication, 1985). Between 1970 and 1980, about 1 million single-room units—nearly one-half of the nation's total—were converted to other uses or destroyed (5). Each of these reductions has severely limited housing opportunities for the mentally ill in the community.

The mentally ill are also at high risk for becoming or remaining homeless because of certain characteristics of their illness (9). Persons who are severely mentally ill are defined as those who have a diagnosis of schizophrenia, manic-depressive illness, organic brain syndrome, or some other type of major mental disorder. A severely mentally disabled person has one or more functional problems, such as the inability to meet basic survival needs, difficulty with the tasks of daily living, extreme vulnerability to stress, the inability to develop or sustain social networks, and lack of motivation or ability to seek out the help of human service workers (10). Because the mentally disabled frequently do not have the skills to negotiate service systems in the community, they are often unable to secure welfare, Social Security benefits, or other entitlements for which they are eligible.

Bassuk notes that the lack of a home may be indicative of an inability to mobilize and to use potential supports, and that such deficits may account, in part, for homelessness among the mentally ill (11). Segal uses the term "social margin" to refer to "all personal possessions, attributes, or relationships which can be traded on for help in time of need" (12). Many people who are mentally ill have difficulty developing social supports, and they do not have the "social margin" that is needed when they are faced with a situation that requires such supports; namely, a housing crisis.

Finally, the "community" plays a specific role in contributing to the severely mentally ill becoming or remaining homeless. The stigma of serious mental illness and its operational sequel, community resistance, create barriers and deny access of the mentally ill to opportunities for housing, jobs, and economic independence that might otherwise exist.

THE RELATIONSHIP BETWEEN DEINSTITUTIONALIZATION AND HOMELESSNESS

Over the past three decades, we have witnessed dramatic changes in the locus of care for the mentally ill that have come about because of changes in clinical practice, newly enacted legal mandates, and changes in public policy (particularly, with respect to mental health financing). In 1955, there were 535,000 psychiatric patients in state hospitals in this country; by 1980, the number had dropped to 132,000. The number is now approximately 126,000 (13).

The vast majority of chronically mentally ill persons who have been discharged from state hospitals are not homeless and live in an array of independent and supervised community residential settings. However, a number of mentally disabled persons do not have access to an adequate number and range of supervised living situations, basic life supports, and other human services essential for their ongoing care, treatment, and rehabilitation in the community. Instead they have been relegated to substandard board and care homes, single-room-occupancy hotels, inappropriate placement in nursing homes—or are without homes and living in emergency shelters, on the streets, or in local jails. More restrictive public psychiatric hospital admissions criteria have also led to an increase in the number of severely mentally ill persons who are being diverted from inpatient hospitalization and being treated in community-based settings. This group of young people, between the ages of 18 and 35, is often referred to as the "young adult chronic population" (14). Although they may not need inpatient care, they often require appropriate residential placement opportunities coupled with supportive services. The problem may be further complicated by the tendency of such persons to resist the structure and rules of traditional facilities and programs.

Because there have not always been adequate community funding, planning, and public support for the severely mentally ill, the implementation and success of deinstitutionalization policy has varied significantly for different states, for different communities, and for different persons. This has led to a backlash against a policy that was never properly implemented and to calls for making civil commitment laws less restrictive. However, when an appropriate system of care is in place for the mentally ill, homelessness does not have to be an outcome of deinstitutionalization. In addition to providing community-based mental health treatment, such a system would provide housing, food, health care, income supports, case management, varying levels of supervision, and, in only a limited number of cases, long-term treatment in an inpatient setting.

WHAT IS BEING DONE TO ADDRESS THE NEEDS OF THOSE WHO ARE HOMELESS?

The problem of homelessness has engendered an outpouring of support from private citizens and organizations (including businesses, local nonprofit groups, churches and synagogues, and other voluntary organizations) in almost every major city across the nation. Typically, groups have set up emergency shelters and food banks, while individuals have cooked meals and accumulated donations of clothes, linens, and funds.

But there have been atypical responses as well. In New York City, the city with "the most pronounced homeless problem in the U.S.," the Road Runners Club began an experimental running and fitness program for residents of city shelters in collaboration with the City Department of Human Resources (15, 16). In Washington, D.C., the American Institute of Architects volunteered its services to redesign a large shelter facility to make the best advantage of the physical plant. The most dramatic example of private sector involvement is provided by the Robert Wood Johnson Foundation and the Pew Memorial Trust; they announced a grant program that made awards of over $25 million to projects in 18 of the nation's most populous cities to develop strategies for providing health care to the homeless (17).

Additionally, at every level of government (federal, state, and local), there have been attempts to respond to the immediate emergency needs of the heterogeneous homeless population (18, 19). Since fiscal year 1983, Congress has appropriated $210 million for emergency shelter and food assistance. These funds are administered through the Federal Emergency Management Agency and the United Way. The funds have provided 85 million meals and 13 million nights of shelter, but observers have noted that the need is 15 to 20 times greater than the aid that has been provided (20).

In October, 1983, then-Secretary of Health and Human Services (HHS) Margaret M. Heckler created a Federal Interagency Task Force on the Homeless (chaired by HHS), including representatives from 12 other federal agencies (21). Its intent is to cut red tape so that existing resources are targeted more effectively toward the problems of the homeless and to act as a broker between local providers of shelter (whether public or private) and the federal government.

Similar initiatives have been forthcoming from state and local governments across the nation. For example, in 1984 alone, New York City spent a record $100 million to provide food and shelter for the growing number of homeless people in the city; that figure does not include services to homeless families and children, nor does it account for the needs of those who live in the street and refuse assistance. Controversy over how to handle leadership responsibility for and the financial burden of addressing the problem of homelessness still remains, however, as each layer of government tends to "pass the buck."

For example, Milwaukee Mayor Henry W. Maier, representing the U.S. Conference of Mayors, noted that local government doesn't have the resources to take on "social overhead problems" and that local taxes are intended to finance "roads, bridges, and garbage pick-up" (17). He went on to state that federal income tax is the "richest tax in the world" and a more appropriate source of revenue for programs for the homeless. New York Governor Mario Cuomo, who chaired the National Governors' Association Task Force on the Homeless, noted, "The dimensions of homelessness are national and they require action at the national level ... we must establish a national housing program for low income individuals and families" (19). And Secretary Margaret Heckler of the Department of Health and Human Services has noted, "Homelessness is essentially a local problem ... the problem originates at the community level and the focus of efforts to resolve it must be made at the same level" (21).

While private and governmental entities struggle with emergency and transitional solutions, the lack of stable, affordable, and more permanent housing opportunities (particularly those linked to support services) still remains the greatest unmet need of the population. Because of the paucity of such living arrangements, candidates for overnight shelters increase, more beds are added to already crowded shelter facilities, and persons remain in interim and transitional shelters because they have no other place to go. In New York City, the average homeless person remains in an emergency shelter for 11 months, and it is acknowledged that those with psychiatric problems stay even longer (22). A one-day "snapshot" study of 922 residents at three city shelters conducted by the New York City Human Resource Administration resulted in the recommendation that greater efforts be made to develop long-term placement alternatives for older and mentally ill shelter residents (23).

In January 1985, a bipartisan Senate-House Task Force on the Homeless was formed to operate as a forum for pursuing information and proposals in order to cut across the wide range and number of ongoing Congressional committees that have conducted hearings, carried out field investigations, and examined solutions to the problem of homelessness (20). A number of proposals, aimed at both immediate and long-term approaches to the problems of the homeless, have been introduced in Congress. In addition, members have sought to extend existing social service programs (for example, SSI) through better outreach efforts.

WHAT SPECIAL EFFORTS HAVE BEEN MADE TO ASSIST THOSE WHO ARE MENTALLY ILL AND HOMELESS?

The homeless mentally ill have obviously benefited from shelter, health, and other social service interventions directed at the broad homeless population. But it is clear that the homeless mentally ill require special attention as well. The mentally ill are often excluded from programs designed to serve the homeless, and those who do not have a fixed address are typically ineligible for necessary mental health services. The number of programs specifically designed to assist those who are both mentally ill and homeless are woefully inadequate in relation to need (24).

Many community mental health programs are so short of staff and underfunded that they are able to serve only those who come to their doors and cannot provide the labor-intensive, skilled outreach that is often necessary to bring the homeless mentally ill in from the streets. On the other hand, emergency shelters generally lack the trained professional mental health staff needed to identify serious psychiatric disorders, develop supportive relationships, provide case management services, and initiate referrals to long-term housing and mental health programs. Thus, the homeless mentally ill often languish in shelters for extended periods of time or are shuttled back and forth between shelters and high-cost emergency rooms and local jails.

Although a growing number of innovative responses have specifically targeted the problems of the homeless mentally ill, these have been the exception rather than the rule. Because of the work of high-energy individuals and coalitions of concerned advocates, specialized programs for the mentally disabled have evolved—most often in the form of mobile outreach programs, case management approaches, drop-in centers, consultation programs to shelter-providers, crisis housing programs, transitional or second-stage housing programs, and long-term residences linked to supportive housing (24).

The fact that so many of the homeless mentally ill on the streets of our cities are not served or are inappropriately served has called attention to the glaring inadequacies of our system of care for the chronically mentally ill and has evoked governmental and organizational responses. In California, for example, bipartisan legislation has been passed to create special social support agencies to provide food, clothing, housing, and mental health services to those who are homeless and mentally ill (25).

In 1983, under the leadership of Dr. John Talbott, the American Psychiatric Association (APA) established a special Task Force on the Homeless Mentally Ill. Chaired by Dr. Richard Lamb, the Task Force developed a comprehensive volume outlining the nature of the problems of the homeless mentally ill and provided recommendations to address those problems (8). In December 1985, the American Public Health Association (APHA) convened a meeting of 14 major mental health constituency groups to share information on current concerns and activities and to discuss future public policy regarding the homeless mentally ill. As an outgrowth of that initial meeting, the organizations decided to meet on an ongoing basis in order to work on the implementation of programs to assist the homeless mentally ill. With leadership from the National Mental Health Association, four subcommittees have been created in the areas of legislative advocacy, research, technical assistance, and public education (26).

Although the National Institute of Mental Health (NIMH) no longer directly funds mental health services, in 1983 it established a focal point for research and technical assistance activities designed to assist states and localities in serving the homeless with severe and persistent mental disorders. Its major effort is directed toward the improvement of the system of treatment and community-based care for the chronically mentally ill in order to avert homelessness. The modestly funded NIMH Community Support Program works with states to improve the system of services for the chronically mentally ill. Any long-term approach to help the homeless mentally ill will require the expansion and improvement of comprehensive systems of housing and financial, medical, mental health, and rehabilitative supports.

A parallel thrust has been to improve our understanding of the characteristics of the homeless mentally ill population, the implications for service delivery, and our knowledge of effective strategies for working with those who are already homeless. Clearly, the mentally ill living in shelters and on the streets are least able to sustain such an existence. In 1983, NIMH awarded seven grants to study the demographic and other characteristics of the homeless mentally ill population (27). In 1985, NIMH supplemented six existing Community Support Project grants to states to provide partial funding support for innovative community-based demonstration projects serving the homeless mentally ill (28).

CONCLUSIONS

Given the high prevalence of mental illness among the homeless, the fact that many of the homeless do not seek out traditional mental health services or other resources on their own, and the paucity of mental health professionals that work in basic shelter programs—the need for competent and experienced mental health professionals to provide services and develop solutions is readily apparent. Responsibility for the nation's homeless mentally ill, however, transcends the mental health community. Many states and communities are developing strategies to help the homeless mentally ill, and there is a growing recognition that comprehensive care for the population must involve collaboration across various levels of government, among housing, mental health and human service agencies, and between the public and private sector. Both the long-term and the immediate emergency needs of this population must be addressed.

As public policy is formulated, mental health professionals can provide necessary leadership in a number of ways: by improving the limited base of available information on the characteristics of the subgroup of the homeless who are mentally ill; by drawing attention to their special treatment, housing, and support needs; by examining the causes of homelessness among the chronically mentally ill; and by assuring that such persons have access to the broad range of community and hospital-based services appropriate to their needs.

In an October 3, 1984, hearing before the House Government Operations Subcommittee on Intergovernmental Relations and

Human Resources, Congressman Ted Weiss poignantly stated, "Homelessness is an epidemic and it is a crisis ... yet we have a more efficient system in the United States to deal with stray pets than we have for homeless human beings" (29). To be mentally ill and homeless offers even fewer options. Some have said, "A simple way to abate homelessness is to reinstitutionalize the mentally ill" (15). The role of the true advocate is less simple—it involves the challenge of expanding and improving community resources and services, while making every effort to protect patients' rights and the dignity of a vulnerable and disabled population.

References

1. Department of Health and Human Services, and Department of Housing and Urban Development: Report on Federal Efforts to Respond to the Shelter and Basic Living Needs of Chronically Mentally Ill Persons. Washington DC, DHHS/DHUD, February 1983

2. *Klosterman v. Cuomo*, New York State Supreme Court, index no 11270/82

3. Department of Housing and Urban Development: A Report to the Secretary on the Homeless and Emergency Shelters. Washington DC, DHUD, 1984

4. Stockdill JW: Testimony Submitted to the Subcommittee on the District of Columbia, Committee on Appropriations, United States Senate, January 23, 1985

5. Department of Health and Human Services: The Homeless: Background, Analysis, and Options. Washington DC, DHHS, August, 1984

6. United States General Accounting Office: Homelessness: Complex Problem and the Federal Response. Washington DC, GAO, April 1985

7. Roth D, Bean J, Lust N, et al: Homelessness in Ohio: A Study of People in Need. Ohio Department of Mental Health, 1985

8. Lamb HR (ed): The Homeless Mentally Ill. Washington DC, American Psychiatric Press, Inc., 1984

9. Levine IS: Homelessness: its implications for mental health policy and practice. Psychosocial Rehabilitation Journal 7:6-16, 1984

10. National Institute of Mental Health: Guidelines for Community Support Systems. Rockville, MD, NIMH, 1977. Revised edition, 1980

11. Bassuk E, Rubin L, Lauriat A: Is homelessness a mental health problem? Am J Psychiatry 141:1546-1549, 1984

12. Segal SP, Baumohl J: Engaging the disengaged: proposals on madness and vagrancy. Social Work 25:358-365, 1980

13. Division of Biometry and Epidemiology: Unpublished surveys of state and county mental hospitals. Rockville, MD, NIMH, 1980

14. Pepper B, Kirshner M, Ryglewicz H: The young adult chronic patient: overview of a population. Hosp Community Psychiatry 32:463-469, 1981

15. Perkins J: New institutions for the homeless. Wall Street Journal, February 26, 1985

16. Road Runners give exercise to homeless. New York Times, March 10, 1985

17. Sinclair M: Homeless to get health care. Washington Post, December 20, 1984

18. Carmody D: The city sees no solutions for homeless. New York Times, October 10, 1984

19. Cuomo M: 1983—Never Again: A report to the National Governors' Association Task Force on the Homeless. Albany, New York State Executive Chamber, 1983

20. Rothman R: Members seek permanent aid for homeless. Congressional Quarterly, March 30, 1985

21. Heckler M: Memorandum on HHS actions to help the homeless. Washington DC, DHHS, 1984

22. Crystal S, Goldstein M: Correlates of shelter utilization: one-day study. New York, Human Resources Administration, 1984

23. McFadden RD: Study of homeless cites special needs. New York Times, September 30, 1984

24. Levine IS: Service programs for the homeless mentally ill, in The Homeless Mentally Ill. Edited by Lamb HR. Washington DC, American Psychiatric Press, Inc., 1984

25. Bronzan B: Dramatic reforms will relieve chaos in California mental health system (press release). Sacramento, California State Assembly, March 18, 1985

26. American Public Health Association: National Leadership workshop on the homeless mentally ill: proceedings of the workshop. Washington DC, APHA, 1985

27. Bachrach L: Report and analytical summary of a meeting of DHHS-supported researchers studying the homeless mentally ill. Rockville, MD, NIMH, 1984

28. Program Guidance: Competing Grant Supplements to Community Support (CSP) Projects Focusing on Chronically Mentally Ill Persons Who are Homeless. Rockville, MD, National Institute of Mental Health, 1985

29. Millions in federal funds for the homeless remain unspent. New York Times, October 4, 1984

2

Mental Illness in the Homeless

Michael J. Vergare, M.D.
A. Anthony Arce, M.D.

2

Mental Illness in the Homeless

During the 1980s, increased attention has been given to the plight of the homeless who are mentally ill. Efforts on the part of advocacy groups, professional groups, and the news media have helped to highlight a growing problem that some view as an outgrowth of the deinstitutionalization of the chronic patient. Concerns about the impact of current national fiscal policies and rising unemployment have added new voices to those expressing alarm.

The forgotten urban drifter has always been present in our cities. Studies have attempted to develop profiles of the kinds of people who are represented in this population, starting with the workhouses of London and the skid rows of large metropolitan cities in the United States. From the 1950s onward, skid rows began to decrease in size in the United States. At the same time, significant changes occurred in the composition of the homeless as growing numbers of deinstitutionalized chronic mental patients found themselves drifting without adequate shelter. In recent years the population described by various authors (1-3) as young adult chronic patients, a group marked by frequent disruptions in

This study was conducted under the auspices of Hahnemann University/JFK Community Mental Health Center, Philadelphia, Pennsylvania.

living arrangements, has also contributed to the ranks of the homeless.

The extent of mental illness among the homeless has been studied by a variety of methods in a wide range of settings (4). The settings have included shelter facilities, psychiatric units, food lines, emergency rooms, and the open streets. Methods have included retrospective record reviews as well as formal observation and formal interviews.

Little research using direct psychiatric observation of the homeless has been reported. A review of the literature underscores the influence that sampling techniques have had in determining the profiles obtained on the population. The lack of consistency found in the results reflects methodological problems that are encountered in studying the homeless population from almost any perspective. These problems are even more critically complex when the focus is on characterizing the mentally ill among the homeless.

THE FIRST STUDY

In 1983 the authors (5) reported on the psychiatric profile of 193 persons (150 men and 43 women) admitted to an emergency shelter in Philadelphia between January and March of 1982. This homeless population was drawn from the streets and included the so-called "vent-men and bag ladies," those who inhabited a small skid-row area or city missions, and those who came to emergency rooms. The sample was drawn from the entire Philadelphia community rather than from any one location. The 193 subjects represented all those admitted to an emergency shelter during a two-month period of severe cold and constituted one-third of the 600 or so persons screened. Screening was done by city welfare department case workers. The sample was a reflection of a procedure that probably excluded persons who did not exhibit gross evidence of psychopathology and thus were acceptable for immediate placement in alternative facilities, such as boarding homes and personal care homes.

Direct psychiatric evaluations were used and supplemented by extended observation. One hundred seventy-nine of the 193 admissions were seen by psychiatrists. *DSM-III* criteria were applied. Mental illness was diagnosed in 151 residents (84 percent). Sixty-seven residents (34.7 percent) had a primary diagnosis of schizophrenia; 44 (22.8 percent), of substance abuse; 12 (6.2 percent), of personality disorder; 10 (5.2 percent), of affective disorder; nine (4.7 percent), of organic brain syndrome; four (2 percent), of mental retardation; and five (2.6 percent), of other disorders. A secondary diagnosis of substance abuse was made in 33 (17 percent) of the subjects. Thus, in total 77 (40 percent) had a major problem with the use of alcohol, drugs, or a combination of both.

Three subgroups were identified based on the duration of their homelessness: the chronically homeless, who regularly lived on the streets (43 percent); the episodically homeless (32 percent), who alternated between being domiciled and not being domiciled for a variable but extended period of time; and the situationally homeless (13 percent), who were usually domiciled but had suddenly been deprived of shelter as a result of an acute personal crisis. No information was available concerning the duration of homelessness in 12 percent of the subjects.

THE SECOND STUDY

A second study was conducted in a new facility in operation from November 1982 to June 1983. The sample consisted of 193 subjects out of a total of 339 unduplicated admissions.

The shelter, which was called the Adult Evaluation Center (AEC), had a resident capacity of 50 with an expected five-day maximum stay. It provided both shelter and evaluation for mental, medical, and social problems and operated in conjunction with other city and private housing alternatives for the homeless.

Residents presented themselves for admission to the City Department of Welfare (DPW) or were referred to DPW for placement. DPW established selection criteria in conjunction with the clinical team placed on site at the AEC. Only clients with a past history of being difficult to place in a residential setting or those who showed evidence of medical illness or psychopathology were considered potential candidates for admission to the AEC. Of the 2,000 or so people screened by DPW, only 17 percent were referred to the AEC. The other 83 percent were referred to a number of social agencies and boarding homes throughout the city. Those who gave evidence of severe acute mental illness were referred to hospital emergency rooms.

Data obtained in the second study were considerably more elaborate than that obtained in the first. Demographic characteristics, such as age, race, mental status, prior mental health contact, and so forth, were recorded at intake by the mental health worker or by social service staff. Information concerning the client's presenting problems, symptomatology, level of functioning, diagnosis, and comprehensive assessment was developed and updated by the psychiatrists. Clinical evaluations and the prescription of treatment for general medical/surgical problems were conducted by the staff internist, or if he or she was not available, by a physician's assistant and a psychiatrist. Clients' progress notes, social service needs, and goals for disposition were recorded by the professional staff. We supplemented all of this information by visiting the Adult Service Division of the Department of Public Welfare to obtain information that might be on record with that department. Through this process we were able to expand the data on referral sources, prior mental health contacts, and occupational status.

FINDINGS

Although the two studies differed in design and in the circumstances of the shelters, the overall profile of the subjects regarding sex, race, and age distribution remained essentially unchanged.

There were, however, significant shifts in the street status of the residents, with a reduction in the number of those deemed chronically homeless—that is, those without identified housing for 30 days or more. The chronically homeless decreased from 43 percent in the first sample to 10 percent in the second sample. The episodically homeless increased from 32 percent to 40 percent and the situationally homeless increased from 13 percent to 50 percent of the overall sample.

New data collected in the second sample included educational status. Sixteen percent had only grade school educations, and 45 percent reported graduating from high school. Only 26 percent reported being military veterans, 82 percent were residents of Philadelphia, and 51 percent reported prior contact with police ranging from misdemeanors to serious crimes. One or more medical problems were found in 52 percent of the population as compared to 22 percent in the first sample. These problems ranged from minor infections to serious cardiac problems, severe diabetes, and hypertension.

There was also an increase in those identified as having had prior mental health contacts. Fifty-nine percent of those in the

Table 1. General Characteristics

	(N = 193) 1982	(N = 193) 1983
Sex		
Male	78	68
Female	22	32
Race		
Black	50	57
White	47	40
Hispanic	3	3
Eurasian	1	—
Age		
18–29	23	27
30–39	24	26
40–49	20	18
50–59	15	14
60 and above	14	16
Unknown	5	0.5
Street Status		
Chronic	43	10
Episodic	32	40
Situational	13	50
Prior Mental Health Contact		
None	59	28
Inpatient	41	60
Outpatient	—	5
Unknown	—	7
Medical Illness		
No Medical Problems	78	48
One or More Medical Problems	22	52

first sample had no reported contact, whereas 65 percent of the second sample reported inpatient or outpatient mental health care in the past. Also noted was a significant increase in length of stay. The group remaining for one week dropped from 63 percent in the first study to 35 percent in the second study. There was a change in referral patterns with fewer residents being referred by police and an increase in those who were self-referred or referred by agencies, social services, and hospitals.

The diagnostic profile of the two populations differed very little. These findings are noted in Table 4. Schizophrenia continued to

Table 2.   General Characteristics: 1983

	Percent
Marital Status	
Never married	57
Married	10
Not residing with spouse	33
Educational Status	
Grade school	16
High school	39
High school graduate	29
Post-high school	16
Veteran	
Yes	26
No	74
Relatives in Philadelphia	
Yes	78
No	22
Police Contact	
Yes	51
No	49

Table 3.   Referral Source

Referral Source	1982		1983	
	N	Percent	N	Percent
Police	68	35.2	17	8.8
Agencies	27	14.0	53	27.5
Self	23	11.9	57	29.5
No information	71	36.8	54	28.0
Totals	189	100.0	181	100.0

be the most frequently recorded diagnosis. There was less substance and alcohol abuse reported as a primary psychiatric diagnosis in the second study. The incidence of dual diagnosis of substance abuse and mental illness was 47 percent.

Medications were prescribed when indicated, but no resident
was forced to take them. In the first sample, 41 percent of the 193
residents were prescribed medication and of that 41 percent, 86
percent complied willingly. In the second sample, 78 percent of
the residents were prescribed medication and all complied. Antipsychotic drugs and anti-Parkinsonian drugs were the primary
medications used, but a large number of residents (22 percent) also
received nonpsychotropic medications.

Discharge placements are summarized in Table 5. In the second
study there was a significant increase in the number of people
leaving without a plan for shelter (from 26 to 60). We believe this
change was consistent with the increased numbers of situationally

Table 4. Primary Psychiatric Diagnosis

Diagnosis	1982		1983	
	N (193)	Percent	N (193)	Percent
Schizophrenia				
Paranoid	23		42	
Other	44		51	
Total	67	34.7	93	48.2
Substance Abuse				
Alcohol	36		17	
Drug	6		1	
Mixed	2		5	
Total	44	22.8	23	11.9
Personality Disorder	12	6.2	21	10.9
Affective Disorder	10	5.2	9	4.7
Other				
Unspecified psychosis	2		4	
Mental retardation	4		3	
Other	3		0	
Total	9	4.7	7	3.6
Organic Brain Syndrome	9	4.7	16	8.3
No mental illness	28	14.5	15	7.8
No information	14	7.2	9	4.6
Totals	193	100.0	193	100.0

homeless, who tended to wander in and out of a variety of placements.

DISCUSSION

The circumstances surrounding the sampling process and the settings in which the two studies were conducted were obviously different. The first study was conducted on the battlefront—in a service setting created virtually overnight in response to an anticipated catastrophe: the possible death of many homeless persons during prolonged record subfreezing weather. Under these conditions the subjects were literally scooped up off the streets and brought to a temporary shelter that had been hastily organized.

This experience led to a series of recommendations for the planned development of a care system which was to be in place the following winter. Services were to be provided through the

Table 5. Discharge Placement

Disposition	N (193)	Percent	N (193)	Percent
Psychiatric Hospital				
Involuntary	9		6	
Voluntary	3		0	
Total	12	6.2	6	3.1
General Hospital	6	3.1	8	4.1
Detoxification Unit	7	3.6	4	2.1
Skilled Nursing Facility	1	0.5	0	0.0
Residential				
Boarding home	67		94	
Home for the aged	15		0	
Foster home	3		0	
Other	4		0	
Total	89	46.1	94	48.7
Family or Friend	20	10.4	8	4.1
Own Recognizance				
With plan for shelter	14		6	
Without plan for shelter	26		60	
Total	40	20.7	66	34.2
Deceased	1	0.5	0	0.0
No information	17	8.8	7	3.6
Totals	193	99.9	193	99.9

planned collaboration of staffs from the Department of Public Welfare (DPW), the Department of Health, and the Community Mental Health Center (CMHC). A fairly detailed operational protocol and a standard medical record were developed. After participating staffs were given orientation, the shelter opened long before a weather emergency. There was no crisis, no urgency. The change in referral patterns—a significant decrease in police referrals coupled with an increase in agency and self-referrals—reflects the difference in these circumstances.

During the second year a Drop-In Center, where no pre-admission screening was needed, was opened. This alternative shelter no doubt influenced the second sample and may account in part for the decrease in the number of chronically homeless in the second sample. However, the mildness of the 1982/83 winter in Philadelphia as compared to the 1981/82 winter may also have had the effect of keeping the chronically homeless from seeking shelter and making shelter space more readily available for the situationally homeless. Although the two samples were drawn from the pool of homeless persons in Philadelphia, a number of intervening variables affected admissions and thus the rigorous comparability of the two samples.

Our analysis of both samples underscores the high prevalence of psychopathology present among the homeless even after they have had the benefit of food, warmth, health care, and a place to sleep. This appears to contradict the view of those who have suggested that the high incidence of psychopathology among the homeless may be a reflection of hunger and sleep deprivation (6). Although any study of the prevalence of psychiatric disorders among the homeless will be affected by the nature of the sampling, our study is of note because of the high incidence of illness in a group who did not present in a traditional hospital or mental health setting. We must keep in mind that at the time of the study, in addition to the shelter and other alternatives described, existing hospital emergency services and outpatient clinics were being used to screen and place homeless persons who were more acutely and severely mentally ill.

Our two studies present a broader picture than that obtained from studies performed in skid row or flophouse environments where there is an over-emphasis on the homeless who are male and alcoholic. Excluded from our studies were homeless families and children. This subgroup of the homeless appears to be increasing as a result of current economic and social problems and warrants further study.

PLANNING FOR SERVICES

The program from which these studies developed reflected a high level of coordination between social, general medical, and specialized psychiatric services in an attempt to evaluate and place those who are homeless and mentally ill. From the experience of this program a number of factors appear to be extremely important for those planning treatment and support programs for the homeless.

Clearly, "street people" constitute a very varied population. It is not a group consisting solely of former state hospital patients who were dumped into communities, although this group does constitute a significant subgroup of the homeless mentally ill. Pepper, Bachrach, and Lamb (1, 2, 3) have each pointed out a group of chronically mentally ill patients who have never been institutionalized—a group that forms an important component of the homeless mentally ill population. The behavior of this group is often more aggressive and demanding than the passive, withdrawn manner of the deinstitutionalized patients. They are more likely to approach a program for service but then maintain contact in an erratic manner. Although this group differs from the image of a street person as an older, chronic schizophrenic, they frequently suffer from severe deficits and require extensive residential and rehabilitative services in conjunction with psychiatric interventions.

Another important finding that has bearing on program development is that shelter residents with diagnosable mental illnesses did improve when adequately treated. Having a psychiatrist and mental health workers on site in the shelter allowed for early intervention that frequently led to treatment compliance. Unfortunately, psychiatric expertise is often not included as a component to shelter work with the homeless mentally ill. Evaluations provided within the context of the shelter are often much more productive and informative than the kind of information that can be obtained by removing a shelter resident to a psychiatric emergency room.

Having mental health services included in the shelter led to a higher degree of compliance with treatment follow-up. A surprisingly high percentage of our shelter residents who were prescribed medications readily accepted them. This acceptance was fostered by a shelter philosophy that was both caring and respectful of the individual's need to make a choice for himself. Our shelter residents knew that they were there to be protected from inclement weather and were free to leave or refuse medication if they so desired. In this type of milieu, residents appear more likely to join staff as partners in their care.

Another important consideration is the high prevalence of physical problems in the population that frequents shelters. We saw in our work problems ranging from dermatitis and frostbite to cardiac decompensation and substance withdrawal. These problems are a routine part of the lives of those who live on urban streets. Ideally, any facility that offers temporary or permanent shelter should have access to suitable medical care.

Another problem that requires careful planning is the placement of clients after their initial sheltering. Although some shelters are designed for long-term care, most must set some limit on length of stay. Careful collaboration between agencies responsible for housing and welfare and agencies responsible for treatment and rehabilitation programs is needed. Unfortunately, in many urban areas such collaboration can prove difficult. Follow-up residential facilities that are attuned to the needs of mental patients must be established to minimize the revolving door syndrome of patients going through community shelters.

The homeless mentally ill present an interesting array of challenges to those who attempt to organize services for them. In some respects they are the last to be served by the community mental health movement. Their plight mirrors the fragmentation that exists in many of our service systems within the community. The programs that we develop to serve them must combine the expertise that was once more commonly offered in a state hospital setting with the flexible, individualized approach found in the better models of community-based care.

References

1. Pepper B, Kirshner MC, Ryglewicz H: The young adult chronic patient: overview of a population. Hosp Community Psychiatry 32:463–469, 1981

2. Bachrach LL: Young adult chronic patients: an analytical review of the literature. Hosp Community Psychiatry 33:189–197, 1982

3. Lamb HR: Young adult chronic patients: the new drifters. Hosp Community Psychiatry 33:465–468, 1982

4. Arce AA, Vergare MJ: Identifying and characterizing the mentally ill among the homeless, in The Homeless Mentally Ill. Edited by Lamb HR. Washington DC, American Psychiatric Association, 1984

5. Arce AA, Tadlock M, Vergare MJ, et al: A psychiatric profile of street people admitted to an emergency shelter. Hosp Community Psychiatry 34:812–817, 1983

6. Hopper K, Baxter E, Cox S, et al: One Year Later: The Homeless Poor in New York City. New York, Community Service Society, 1982

3

Characteristics and Service Needs of the Homeless Mentally Ill

Frank Lipton, M.D.
Albert Sabatini, M.D.
Peter Micheels, M.A.

3

Characteristics and Service Needs of the Homeless Mentally Ill

Although homelessness among the mentally ill is not a new phenomenon, the scope and nature of the problem have changed dramatically over the past several years. The homeless mentally ill are a heterogeneous group of persons including representatives from the young adult chronic population, the criminalized, the recidivist, and other chronically impaired groups (1, 2, 3). Rather than emphasizing those features which differentiate members of the group, it is more useful, from a planning perspective, to examine those characteristics which they all share. The homeless mentally ill generally suffer from a chronic illness which may be biological, psychological, or both. In addition, most lack any form of stable social network or support system (4). The differentiating labels applied to various subgroups within the chronic population are often the result of describing the same person at different times during his or her life cycle, or in different places—whether it be in a hospital, in prison, or on the streets.

In 1982 at the American Psychiatric Association Meeting in Toronto, we reported the results of a study of 90 homeless patients who presented to the Psychiatric Emergency Service at Bellevue Hospital (5). Of the sample, 96.7 percent had a history of at least one psychiatric hospitalization and 58.9 percent had been in a state hospital. The major diagnostic groups were schizophrenia, accounting for 72.2 percent of the sample, and personality disorders, accounting for 12.2 percent. It was our impression that the sample represented a skewed population as we were examining only those homeless persons who presented to an acute psychiatric service. In the present study we continued to examine the problem but focused instead on a group of homeless persons who appeared at the medical emergency services of Bellevue Hospital.

PROCEDURE

All subjects were first given an interview to obtain information about their economic and social problems and their history of psychiatric hospitalization. A modified version of the Diagnostic Interview Schedule (DIS; Robins, Helzer, Croughan, et al. 1981) was then administered. The DIS was modified by eliminating the questions about somatization disorder, anxiety disorders, and sexual dysfunction. Additional information about the subjects' medical conditions and dispositions were subsequently obtained from their ER charts and any available inpatient records.

The interviews were administered by a group of 10 volunteers, who were trained to use the DIS. The interviews took place through the week, during the day and evening shifts, depending on the availability of an interviewer. On a number of occasions no "homeless" patients were available in the ER. The interviews were conducted over a two-month period from February 1983 to March 1983.

Independent diagnoses using *DSM III* criteria were then made from the DIS protocols by two experienced clinicians. When a patient had a previous Bellevue psychiatric chart, this was examined to corroborate the diagnosis. Subjects were considered to be homeless if they had no address (n = 30), or if they were living at one of the shelters (n = 20).

RESULTS

Subjects were 40 males and 10 females who appeared in a municipal hospital adult emergency room for medical treatment and agreed to be interviewed. Thirty-four of the subjects were white, 11, black, and five, hispanic. Only eight patients were less than 30 years old. Sixty-two percent of the sample were 39 or older and 20 percent were 60 or older. Fifty-six percent of the patients inter- viewed had never married and 94 percent were presently not married.

Forty-four percent of the subjects had completed high school. Of those, 16 percent completed college. Fifty-six percent of the sub- jects failed to complete high school.

A noteworthy feature of this sample is the high percentage of subjects who had not held a job in more than five years: 56 percent had not worked in more than five years and 8 percent had never held a job. Fourteen percent had not been employed for two to five years. Ninety-six percent of the sample were presently unem- ployed. The extent of vocational impairment in this sample is consistent with that reported by other groups, including the New York State Office of Mental Health.

The chronicity of homelessness among this group is striking. Thirty-six percent of the patients in the sample had not had a permanent address for more than five years. Only 30 percent of the sample had been homeless for less than six months. Major reasons patients reported for leaving their permanent residence included eviction (18 percent), lack of funds (26 percent), and personal conflicts (18 percent).

Regarding the utilization of available community resources, it is important to note that 56 percent of the subjects had no source of income. Sixteen percent were receiving SSI, six percent were re- ceiving welfare, and eight percent were receiving Social Security benefits. It is also worth noting that 70 percent of the sample were not receiving any form of health insurance. Only 16 percent were receiving either medicaid or medicare, and although 32 percent of the sample were veterans, only two percent reported receiving veterans' benefits.

Fifty percent of the sample had a history of at least one psychi- atric hospitalization. In four percent of the cases, prior history of psychiatric hospitalization could not be determined. Forty-two percent of the subjects had a history of state hospitalization.

Twenty-six percent of the sample had a history of psychiatric hospitalization in a non-state hospital facility.

Thirty-eight percent of the sample were diagnosed as suffering from a major psychiatric illness with 18 percent receiving a diagnosis of schizophrenia, 16 percent, a diagnosis of a major affective disorder, and four percent, a diagnosis of chronic organic brain syndrome. The incidence of schizophrenia was much lower than we had anticipated on the basis of our previous study. Sixteen percent of the sample received a diagnosis of both alcoholism and a major psychiatric disorder. A surprising number of patients were suffering from alcohol, drug dependence, or both. Only four percent of the sample had no gross pathology.

DISCUSSION

The results of the study make it apparent that a significant number of homeless patients at Bellevue were suffering from some form of chronic mental illness. Many were not utilizing or could not gain access to existing community resources; 57 percent had no source of income; only 20 percent had public health insurance; and only 40 percent reported using city shelters.

Our findings vary with those reported by the New York State Office of Mental Health in their May 1982 report, "Who Are the Homeless?" (6). The population they described included a group of younger men, mainly black and hispanic, of whom only one-third had histories of psychiatric hospitalization and 20 percent had histories of hospitalization in a state facility. The patients in our study were clearly older, predominantly white, and had a greater incidence of psychiatric illness and hospitalizations. An explanation for this discrepancy may be that the older, white, more vulnerable homeless patients cannot fend for themselves in the present shelter system and are being pushed into the streets by the younger, more streetwise group. It has been observed at the shelters that the younger, more able-bodied and aggressive males will prey on the older, more defenseless men.

Data from the study also indicate that the municipal hospital system has become an integral part of skid row and is being used by many of the homeless to obtain a variety of services in addition to medical care. The respondents in the study reported using the hospital to get out of the cold, to get rest, to get a place to sleep, to get food, to get a subway token. The hospitals are functioning as soup lines, hotels, shelters, and rest stops and seem to provide more comprehensive services in a safer environment.

The high incidence of alcoholism found in this study sample indicates that the alcoholic has not vanished from skid row. In this regard it is important to remember that alcoholism is a chronic illness and that a significant percentage of alcoholics become sufficiently disabled or disturbed so as to become involved in the mental health care system.

While for some the state of homelessness may be a temporary phenomenon arising from an acute stressful life event, such as eviction, loss of income, or a catastrophic occurrence, for many homelessness has become a chronic life style. To adequately understand the problem of homelessness, two major issues must be considered: 1) chronicity of impairment within the population, and 2) the systems designed to treat such long-standing disability.

Chronicity, whether it is secondary to medical, psychiatric, or degenerative processes, seems to be a relatively common feature in the evolution of the homeless state. Whatever variations exist in reports on the homeless, one of the most consistent findings is the high incidence of chronic mental illness within the population. A chronic condition may be characterized by long duration, by frequent recurrence over time, and often by slowly progressing impairment. The population of the chronically mentally ill is best defined by diagnosis rather than by duration of hospitalization. Psychiatric diagnoses considered to be chronic conditions, even though the manifestations of the illness may not be apparent at all times, include schizophrenia, major affective disorders, alcoholism, mental retardation, organic brain syndromes, and certain drug addictions and personality disorders. Chronicity can be viewed as the final common pathway for a variety of syndromes resulting from biological, psychological, sociological, or economic processes, acting in isolation or in conjunction. Homelessness can, in part, be viewed as a symptom of chronic disability. By conceptualizing homelessness in this manner, one can understand how skid row has become the repository for the alcoholic, the medically infirm, the aged, the criminal, the unemployed, and the psychotically impaired.

Our inability to provide a useful social function for such persons leaves them lost to wander like vagabonds. Our social system has not developed a means of reintegrating these individuals into the community. The traditional role of the family in caring for the sick and dependent has, to a large extent, been usurped by institutions such as hospitals, nursing homes, and prisons. In *Haven in a Heartless World*, Christopher Lasch has pointed to the diminishing role of the family and to the expanding role of societal structures in managing the handicapped (7). In the past the chronically ill were segregated from the community in state hospitals often located far from the community in which the patient had previously resided. In an attempt to implement a more humanistic treatment approach, the policy of deinstitutionalization was formulated.

The argument that deinstitutionalization is one of the major causes of homelessness is an extremely sensitive one and has been misinterpreted. Although the data clearly indicate that a significant percentage of the homeless have histories of state hospitalization and that many were discharged during the past 10 to 15 years, a significant percentage of homeless people have never been hospitalized and have developed psychiatric disabilities in the postdeinstitutionalization era. These persons, often referred to as the "new young adult chronic patients," have recently been receiving increasing attention (8, 9). The "new" young adult chronic patient may not be new at all—he or she may be an epiphenomenon of the changes within the mental health care delivery system, as the homeless mentally ill are.

It is important to emphasize that deinstitutionalization in itself is not the problem, but the manner in which it was implemented is (10). Inherent in the policy of deinstitutionalization was the development of networks of community services which would facilitate the readjustment and rehabilitation of discharged patients in the community. This network rarely was sufficiently constructed. Whatever condemnation can be made of aspects of the state hospital system, it should be noted that it was a "real system." Food, shelter, clothing, work, and a variety of therapeutic modalities were provided for patients under the auspices of a single organizational structure that assumed total responsibility and was accountable for the results achieved at the institution.

In enacting the policies of deinstitutionalization, we partially abandoned this system (its deficiencies aside). The system, or nonsystem, we adopted never received adequate planning or funding. We are left with a system which provides fragmented services by multiple, often antagonistic providers, who lack any coordinating, organizing responsibility. Trevor Glenn notes that over the past 225 years we have come full circle and states, "we have the most poorly organized system of care since we started with almshouses in 1750."

Chronic homeless patients are among the victims of this failure. The present system of mental health care delivery does not adequately address the needs of this population. The importance of providing food, shelter, and clothing for this group cannot be underestimated. Efforts to improve the quality and quantity of shelter space within the community must continue. However, consideration should also be given to the existence of certain subgroups among the homeless whose survival needs are not being met by the present shelter system. We have delineated a more vulnerable population which is older, manifests a high incidence of psychiatric disability, and is not using the shelter system. Shelter facilities which are more protective and are able to provide not only for survival needs but also medical, psychiatric, and social services in a less threatening milieu must be developed. Providing shelter is not sufficient in and of itself. It is a short-term, "finger-in-the-dike" approach that addresses the problem of homelessness at the most superficial and tentative level.

In *The Homeless Mentally Ill* we have described eight types of support services required to meet the short- and long-term needs of this population (11). Resource development for the homeless mentally ill begins with contact services and shelter and subsequently progresses to residential, financial, psychiatric, and rehabilitative services; all of which must be interconnected and fostered by supportive governmental policies (4).

Contact Services

As noted earlier, the chronic patient is often unable to avail himself or herself of existing services because of disorganization, distrust, or disability. Therefore, contact services are an essential first step in engaging this population (12). Outreach programs can make contact with the homeless on their own turf in a non-demanding and nonthreatening fashion in order to facilitate the formation of trusting relationships. Drop-in centers, soup kitchens, emergency shelters, and multiservice centers are effective modalities through which contact can be made and portals of entry into the system made more accessible. Such programs or facilities must be adequately staffed with multidisciplinary teams capable of assessing the varied needs of the patient population and linking them with the existing network of resources. Case management services are mandatory for every patient to assist in the implementation of the prescribed treatment plan and in order to ensure linkage among service providers.

Shelters

Although emergency shelters are essential in providing the homeless with food, clothing, and shelter, they are of questionable therapeutic value and should be used only as a temporary measure. Nonetheless, shelters are important sites in which to make "contact" with the homeless and may constitute a first stage in the process of rehabilitation and resettlement.

Today's shelters are often overcrowded, understaffed, and ill equipped to provide any services beyond food, clothing, and temporary shelter. Because of the paucity of community residential alternatives, it is extremely difficult for shelters to provide longer-term care.

It is recommended that shelters be limited in size and that they house limited numbers of persons for brief time periods while transitional or long-term placement is being arranged. Certain persons, particularly the homeless mentally ill, will require greater protection and supervision as well as concurrent medical or psychiatric care.

Residential Alternatives

Community residential facilities are the cornerstone of any system designed to focus on the needs of the homeless chronic patient. The lack of appropriate housing is undoubtedly the most critical unmet need of the chronic psychiatric patient (13). If we plan to meet the varying residential needs of this population, a continuum of living arrangements must exist, ranging from highly structured and supervised settings to more autonomous living arrangements. Patients should be placed in those settings which are most likely to facilitate the resident's attainment of his highest adaptive capacity. Ideally, it is preferable to create a rehabilitative focus in the development of such residential settings. To be practical, one must keep in mind that not all patients will be amenable to such an approach and that certain residential facilities will be therapeutic environments, while others will be supportive or custodial in nature (4).

A variety of interrelated barriers to the development of community residential supports include the lack of a standard nomenclature, the lack of a well defined government policy, a paucity of research investigating which settings are likely to be most effective, and community resistance to the development of such settings.

Financial Support

While many homeless persons have no financial support at all, the level of disability of most homeless mentally ill patients is usually substantial enough to warrant Supplemental Security Income (SSI) or Social Security Disability Insurance (SSDI). Several recent studies have noted that a significant number of veterans are included in this population, and that at the same time, very few of these veterans are receiving the benefits they deserve (14).

Health insurance is a crucial support, yet most homeless mentally ill persons have no medical insurance. As a result, they are excluded from treatment in most voluntary and private facilities, some of which would treat the chronic patient if insurance was available. Reimbursement schedules which consider the multiple service needs of those living in the community must be devised.

Those income maintenance, health insurance, and food stamp programs which do exist often have eligibility criteria which exclude this population by frequently requiring proof of residence and a mailing address in order to qualify. In addition, the amount of money allotted through many of these programs is generally inadequate to allow anyone to live in a humane fashion. Financial needs should be reassessed and more realistic allowances developed.

On another level, in order to fund a functional service system for the homeless chronic patient, it will be necessary to tap the resources of a variety of health and human service agencies. The formation of a multi-agency commission which would be authorized to fund programs and oversee service delivery should be considered in constructing an adequate foundation of supports.

Psychiatric Supports

The homeless chronic patient often requires periods of acute psychiatric hospitalization for stabilization (5). As evidenced by overly stringent admitting criteria which require that a patient be seriously decompensated or dangerous to himself or others, by premature discharges with inadequate dispositional planning dictated by an overpressurized system and by frequent emergency room overcrowding, there is a short-term need for increased numbers of acute care beds. Furthermore, intermediate- and chronic-care beds will continue to be a necessity for some chronic patients, no matter how flexible or comprehensive our treatment approach is.

Of equal importance is the availability of other nonhospital-based psychiatric services through which a patient can be ensured of having ongoing contact with a psychiatrist, who can monitor his status and prescribe appropriate treatments.

Rehabilitation

Anthony emphasized the importance of assessing each patient's skills and deficiencies in a variety of settings, including work, living, and social situations (15). An individual rehabilitation program can be formulated based on such an assessment.

For patients unable to attend to fundamental aspects of living, such as personal hygiene, keeping house, cooking, or managing funds, training in skills of daily living is essential. For those who have these basic skills but lack skills needed for vocational and social functioning, socialization programs, social clubs, and activity programs within a residence can enhance independence and the development of interpersonal relationships. Subsequently, vocational training, sheltered workshops, and transitional employment could complete the rehabilitation process.

Case Management

An ideal system would have built into it linkages among service providers in order to ensure integrated and continuous care. In light of the fragmentation in our present care system, it becomes mandatory to create such connections by assigning each patient a case manager who can link the patient with the designated services and coordinate his care (16). Case management is an essential function which can be performed by family members, friends, coworkers, professionals, paraprofessionals, or through the use of interagency meetings.

Governmental, Legal, and Societal Supports

Factors contributing to the obstruction of the development of a unified service delivery system include lack of leadership in the formulation of policy, deficiencies in funding, community opposition, and legal barriers (14).

Agencies at different governmental levels disagree about who should be responsible for the care of the chronically mentally ill, homeless, and otherwise. While cities squabble with states and social service agencies debate with mental health agencies, the homeless mentally ill remain unassisted; the magnitude of the problems of the underprivileged and disadvantaged are minimized by present-day federal initiatives, and the development of a humane social policy is delayed. Some locales pour millions of dollars into the formation of massive shelters which offer little more than short-term solutions. Representatives from the public, private, and voluntary sectors must begin to cooperatively develop an acceptable long-term action plan designed to care for the chronically disabled in an integrated and continuous fashion.

Mental health policy makers should be given access to monies from federal, state, local, and private agencies to permit the development of a full service system capable of providing comprehensive care for the chronic psychiatric patient. Multiple agencies will need to target funds to provide for the diverse needs of the chronic patient. Offices of health, mental health, social services, housing, and labor will need to combine forces if community psychiatry is ever to become a viable modality of treatment. Legal, financial, and social barriers must be torn down. Just as patients have the right to treatment in a hospital, they have the right to treatment in the community. The judicial system must recognize this right and reevaluate legal decisions which impede the provision of humane care to the chronically disabled (17). Stigmas leading to community ignorance and opposition must be tackled head on. For it is not until the community accepts the patient, that the patient will be able to live humanely within the community.

References

1. Bachrach LL: The homeless mentally ill and mental health services: an analytical review of the literature, in The Homeless Mentally Ill. Edited by Lamb HR. Washington DC, American Psychiatric Association, 1984

2. Lamb HR, Grant RW: The mentally ill in an urban county jail. Arch Gen Psychiatry 39:17–22, 1982

3. Goldfinger SM, Hopkin JT, Surber RW: Treatment resisters or system? toward a better service system for acute care recidivists. New Directions for Mental Health Services 21:17–27, 1984

4. Lipton FR, Sabatini A: Constructing support systems for homeless chronic patients, in The Homeless Mentally Ill. Edited by Lamb HR. Washington DC, American Psychiatric Association, 1984

5. Lipton FR, Sabatini A, Katz SE: Down and out in the city: the homeless mentally ill. Hosp Community Psychiatry 34:818–821, 1983

6. New York State Office of Mental Health: Who are the homeless?, in Homelessness in America. Washington DC, U.S. Government Printing Office, 1983

7. Lasch C: Haven in a Heartless World. New York, Basic Books, 1977

8. Bachrach LL: Young adult chronic patients: an analytical review of the literature. Hosp Community Psychiatry 32:463–469, 1981

9. Pepper B, Kirschner MC, Ryglewicz H: The young adult chronic patient: overview of a population. Hosp Community Psychiatry 32:463–469, 1981

10. Lamb HR: Deinstitutionalization and the homeless mentally ill, in The Homeless Mentally Ill. Edited by Lamb HR. Washington DC, American Psychiatric Association, 1984

11. Lamb HR (Ed): The Homeless Mentally Ill: A Task Force Report of the American Psychiatric Association. Washington DC, American Psychiatric Association, 1984

12. Leach J, Wing J: Helping Destitute Men. London, Tavistock Publishers, 1980

13. U.S. Department of Health and Human Services, and U.S. Department of Housing and Urban Development: Report on Federal Efforts

to Respond to the Shelter and Basic Living Needs of Chronically Mentally Ill Individuals. Washington DC, Department of Health and Human Services, February 1983

14. City of New York, Office of the Comptroller, Research and Liaison Unit: Soldiers of Misfortune: Homeless Veterans in New York City, Nov. 1982

15. Anthony WA: Psychological rehabilitation: a concept in need of a method. Am J Psychol 32:658–662, 1977

16. Talbott JA, Lamb HR: Summary and recommendations, in The Homeless Mentally Ill. Edited by Lamb HR. Washington DC, American Psychiatric Press, Inc., 1984

17. Peele R, Gross B, Arons B, et al: The legal system and the homeless, in The Homeless Mentally Ill. Edited by Lamb HR. Washington DC, American Psychiatric Press, Inc., 1984

4

Psychosocial Profiles of the Urban Homeless

Billy E. Jones, M.D.
Beverly A. Gray, M.A.
Deborah B. Goldstein, Ph.D.

4

Psychosocial Profiles of the Urban Homeless

The current research and media focus on the homeless is the result of the dramatic increase in this segment of the population in the past decade. Unfortunately, the extent of homelessness is not clearly documented. A recent article in the *Journal of the American Medical Association* estimated that there are now two million homeless nationwide—as many as there were during the depression of the 1930s (1). On May 1, 1984, the federal Department of Housing and Urban Development issued a report which they called "the first national profile of the homeless," stating that there are only 250,000 homeless nationwide. This figure is much smaller than previous estimates, and some groups feel that it underestimates the actual number of the homeless (2).

New York City has an estimated 36,000 homeless (3). As of April 1984, the city was able to house only 6,500 persons in its 18 shelters (4). In New York, 2,900 families, including 6,500 children, are without homes and are currently being sheltered in welfare hotels (5). New York City will allocate $120 million this year to care for the homeless (4). These statistics highlight the magnitude of the problem of urban homelessness today.

The unprecedented rise in the number of indigent persons can be traced to several factors. Federal budget cuts and the reduction of social welfare programs have caused the economic decline of financially marginal persons. Budget cuts have curtailed the construction of new low-cost housing. Concurrently the existing supply of low-cost housing is being diminished. The process of neighborhood gentrification is eliminating single rooms-only hotels. Long-term tenants are often harassed by landlords who want to charge higher rents. There is no alternative housing which the poor can afford. The New York City Housing Authority estimates that 17,000 families are now "doubling up" in the projects because of the critical shortage in low-cost housing (5). A third major factor in the rise of homelessness is the failure of the deinstitutionalization of the mentally ill. Approximately 6,200 discharged mental patients are homeless in New York City (6).

At Bellevue, the number of hospitalized homeless patients more than doubled in three years, from 14 percent of all hospitalizations in 1978 to more than 30 percent in 1982 (7). The desperate circumstances of the deinstitutionalized homeless prompted a class action suit against the state. In March 1984, New York State's highest court ruled that patients had the right to sue the state to obtain continued housing and care.

Much has been written about the deinstitutionalized homeless, and several major studies give the impression that the homeless are mainly psychotics who are too alienated and disoriented to be able to accept aid (8). However, it is becoming increasingly evident that the homeless are not a homogeneous group of former mental patients. The federal report issued recently stated that the homeless are a heterogeneous group in terms of race, age, sex, and duration of unemployment. The data do not support the old stereotype of the homeless person as a white, middle-aged, alcoholic man. It also disputes the new stereotype of the homeless person as a florid psychotic who is unable to relate to others (2).

Homeless persons with no history of psychiatric hospitalization were surveyed for the present study. A profile of the homeless person who is not identified as mentally ill was sought. Demographic and psychosocial information was collected through the use of self-report measures which were thought to be appropriate for this population. A recent study by Bahr and Houts, which found that homeless men were not more likely than other populations to give discrepant survey information (9), supports the validity of obtaining survey data from the homeless.

The failure of social interventions with the homeless has been attributed to a lack of consideration for the heterogeneity of the target population. It is hoped that this chapter will provide needed information about the diversity of the homeless population and thus will facilitate appropriate care.

METHODOLOGY

Homeless persons were approached and interviewed on a one-to-one basis in the streets and shelters of Manhattan by staff psychologists and social workers from the Department of Psychiatry at Lincoln Medical and Mental Health Center in the Bronx, New York. Criteria for inclusion in the study were as follows: subjects had to be between the ages of 18 and 65, with no history of psychiatric hospitalization and no permanent residence. If a subject fit these criteria, he or she was given the reading subtest of the Wide Range Achievement Test (WRAT) as a literacy check to ensure that he or she would be able to complete the measures which were subsequently administered—Gough's Adjective Checklist and a psychosocial survey developed by the authors.

Psychosocial Survey

The psychosocial survey developed by the authors is a self-report measure consisting of 97 questions requiring forced-choice or open-ended responses. Some of the open-ended items required a yes/no response, and 40 items were on a Likert Scale with the following response choices: "never," "sometimes," "often," or "always." The 40 items were clinical in nature, and they were presented to subjects as "problems." Subjects were asked to tell how often they had each problem. Additionally, one clinical item was presented in checklist form—a list of 21 "severe fears."

All of the clinical items were organized by the authors into symptom clusters to facilitate reporting of results. The symptom clusters were as follows: Neurosis, Psychosis, Organicity, Affective Symptoms, Substance Abuse, Phobias, Suicide, and Aggression-frustration. Questions were included to determine orientation to time, person, and place. The psychosocial survey also asked questions about socioeconomic information including circumstances precipitating homelessness, extent of social networks, and sexual, family, educational, medical, and employment histories. Questions on history of victimization (rape or other physical assault) were also included.

Gough's Adjective Checklist

Gough's Adjective Checklist is a self-report measure consisting of a list of 300 adjectives. Subjects were asked to check those adjectives which they felt were self-descriptive. The adjectives are organized into 37 subscales, which are in turn organized into five clusters by content. Results of the ACL will be reported in another paper.

Statistical Analysis

Frequency distributions were done on the psychosocial survey data. Additionally, correlation co-efficients were calculated between selected items on the psychosocial survey and selected subscales of the ACL. Pearson's correlation co-efficient was used for this purpose. Primarily, psychosocial survey results and correlations between the psychosocial survey and the ACL will be discussed.

RESULTS

Demographic Data

A total of 158 homeless persons were interviewed for our study. Ninety-four (59 percent) were men and 64 (41 percent) were women. A majority (55 percent) were black and 30 percent were caucasians (see Table 1). Thirty-four percent ($N = 54$) were be-

tween the ages of 18 and 29, and another 29 percent ($N = 46$) were
between the ages of 30 and 39. More than one-fourth (27 percent)
($N = 43$) were high school graduates and 14 percent had some
college experience ($N = 22$). Six percent ($N = 9$) were college graduates.

Sociological Data

Homeless State.   Forty-nine percent ($N = 72$) of the subjects
had a permanent residence less than a year before. Another 34
percent ($N = 46$) had a permanent residence one to three years

Table 1.   Demographic Profile of New Homeless, $N = 158$

	N	Percent
Sex		
M	94	59
F	64	41
Race or Ethnic Group		
Black	87	55
Caucasian	47	30
Hispanic or other	22	14
American Indian	2	1
Age Range		
18–29	54	34
30–39	46	29
40–49	25	16
50–59	20	13
60–65	13	8
Marital Status		
Never married	94	59
Married	24	15
Divorced	28	18
Widowed	4	3
Separated or no response	8	5
Educational Level		
Elementary school	12	8
Some high school	58	36
High school graduate	43	27
Some college	22	14
College graduate	9	6
Technical training	1	.06
No response	13	8

before (see Table 2). Thirty-nine percent of the subjects lost their homes for financial reasons. Other subjects (49 percent) lost their homes because of fire or hospitalization, or because their homes were condemned. A majority (63 percent) had been in New York City for more than 11 years.

Employment Experiences.   A majority of the subjects (91 percent) had been employed, with 61 percent employed in unskilled labor. Fifty percent had lost their jobs as a result of being fired or laid off (see Table 3). A majority of the subjects claimed they had had no serious trouble with their co-workers (87 percent) or with their bosses (82 percent).

Table 2.   Questions on Homelessness, N = 158

	N	Percent
1. How long ago did you have a permanent residence or place of your own?		
a. Never	4	2
b. Less than one year	72	49
c. One to three years	46	34
d. Over three years	24	15
	146	100
2. How did you lose your last home?		
a. Financial reasons	61	39
b. Death	4	2
c. Marital or other separation	8	5
d. Other (includes fire, hospitalization, housing condemned, etc.)	78	49
	151	95
3. Where do you sleep now?		
a. Shelter	96	60
b. Street	24	15
c. Friends'	2	1
d. Other (church, community organizations)	27	17
	149	93
4. How long have you been in New York City?		
a. Zero to two years	42	27
b. Three to five years	9	6
c. Six to ten years	5	3
d. More than 11 years	99	63
	155	99

Social Affiliation and Interaction.   Twenty-seven percent of the subjects (*N* = 43) had serious trouble getting along with their family while growing up. Eight percent had trouble getting along with classmates in school, 35 percent played hooky, and 11 percent had serious trouble getting along with their teachers (see Table 4). Eighty-eight percent of the subjects had living relatives, and a majority (78 percent) knew the whereabouts of their relatives. However, only 57 percent had contact with their relatives. A majority of the subjects (68 percent) had friends, but only 51 percent had someone to whom they could turn for help (see Table 4).

Abuse and Assault Experiences.   Almost one-fourth (23 percent) of the subjects were victims of child abuse, and almost one-half (11 percent) of the child abuse was sexual in nature. Forty-nine percent of the subjects had been physically assaulted as an adult (see Table 5). Twenty percent of the subjects were victims of rape. Of this 20 percent (*N* = 32), eight were men and 24 were women. A majority of the subjects (59 percent) were not afraid of being attacked on the street. Sixty-five percent—a majority—were not afraid of being attacked in a shelter.

Table 3.   Employment Experience of New Homeless, *N* = 158

	N	Percent
1. Have you ever been employed?		
a. Yes	143	91
b. No	11	7
2. If yes, what types of work have you done?		
a. Unskilled labor	97	61
b. Skilled technical work	49	31
3. Why did you leave your last job?		
a. Involuntary (fired/laid off)	79	50
b. Voluntary (resigned, personal reasons)	56	35
4. Did you have serious trouble getting along with co-workers on your job?		
a. Yes	10	6
b. No	137	87
5. Did you have serious trouble getting along with your boss on the job?		
a. Yes	19	12
b. No	129	82

**Table 4. Social Affiliation and Interaction of New
Homeless, N = 158**

	N	Percent
1. Did you have serious trouble getting along with your family when you were growing up?		
a. Yes	43	27
b. No	113	72
2. Do you have any living relatives?		
a. Yes	140	88
b. No	15	9
3. If yes, do you know the whereabouts of your relatives?		
a. Yes	124	78
b. No	21	13
4. Do you have any contact with your relatives?		
a. Yes	91	57
b. No	61	39
5. Do you have any friends?		
a. Yes	107	68
b. No	50	32
6. Is there any person that you go to when you need help?		
a. Yes	81	51
b. No	73	46
7. Did you have serious trouble getting along with classmates in school?		
a. Yes	13	8
b. No	142	90
8. Did you have serious trouble getting along with teachers?		
a. Yes	17	11
b. No	138	87
9. Did you play hooky a lot?		
a. Yes	55	35
b. No	102	64

Clinical Results

Before reporting the clinical results, it is important to qualify any clinical interpretation. One must consider the extraordinary environmental conditions of the homeless. For instance, the clinical items that were experienced with the greatest frequency by respondents (see Table 6) clearly involve environmental factors. It would be ludicrous to interpret "trouble getting to sleep" as a psychosomatic symptom for this sample for obvious reasons—they have nowhere to sleep. As the standard deviation of 0.90

indicates, a significant number of respondents ($N = 33$) said they often or always had trouble getting to sleep.

"Feel sad" had the highest mean of any clinical item. Only 26 of the 158 respondents said that they never felt sad. The mean for "feel depressed" was also high. These were the only affective items with means above 1.90. Two other affective items should be mentioned even though their means were not above 1.90—"having racing thoughts" (mean = 1.68, SD = 0.85) and "moods shift quickly" (mean = 1.89, SD = 0.79). A substantial number of respondents reported that they often or always experienced these symptoms. Twenty-two people reported that they often or always had rapid mood shifts. Thus the affective cluster items had striking scatter or deviation in scores, even though most respondents did not experience the symptoms.

The aggression/frustration cluster had the most item means above 1.90. Three items were experienced with relatively high frequency as shown on Table 6. These items were "feel very frustrated," "feel very irritable," and "people get on your nerves a lot."

Table 5. **Responses on Abuse and Assault of New Homeless, $N = 158$**

	N	Percent
1. As a child were you a victim of child abuse?		
a. Yes	36	23
b. No	122	77
2. If yes, was the abuse sexual in nature?		
a. Yes	17	11
b. No	19	12
3. Have you ever been physically assaulted as an adult?		
a. Yes	78	49
b. No	80	50
4. Have you been a victim of rape?		
a. Yes	32	20
b. No	94	59
5. Are you afraid of being attacked on the street?		
a. Yes	62	39
b. No	94	59
6. Are you afraid of being attacked in a shelter?		
a. Yes	55	34
b. No	103	65

Table 6. Clinical Items with Highest Mean Response,
N = 158

Item Number	Mean	SD
50. Trouble getting to sleep	1.96	0.90
54. Feel nervous	1.92	0.81
56. Feel sad*	2.12	0.80
65. People get on your nerves a lot**	2.09	0.79
67. Feel very frustrated**	1.99	0.76
68. Feel very irritable**	1.90	0.75
81. Feel depressed*	2.07	0.82

* Affective Item Cluster
** Aggression/Frustration Item Cluster

Two suicide questions were asked: one to assess current suicidal ideation and one for history of attempt (see Table 7). Only one respondent said that he always felt so sad that he wanted to kill himself, and one said that he often felt that way. Thirty-six persons responded "sometimes," and 120 responded "never." The rate of "never" and "sometimes" responses was consistent for men and women, with 24 percent of men and 23 percent of women sometimes having suicidal ideation; history of attempted suicide, however, was higher for women (20 percent) than for men (15 percent). Twenty-seven people, or 17 percent of the total sample, reported past suicide attempts.

Seventy-two percent of the sample said that they never took drugs, while only 52 percent said they never drank heavily. It is apparent from the SD of 1.06 on the drinking item that quite a few respondents have serious drinking problems. Twenty men and one woman reported drinking heavily all the time, seven men and two women responded "often," and 29 men and 14 women responded that they sometimes drank heavily.

The means and standard deviations for the psychotic item cluster were not particularly noteworthy; that is, no mean was above 1.90 and no standard deviation was above 0.90. However, the psychosis items were of particular interest, and it seemed important to report the percentages of respondents who experienced these symptoms with any frequency at all (Table 8). Substantial percentages of the sample reported that they sometimes experienced depersonalization (question 51) and derealization (question 58). Question 59 probed for paranoid ideation, but considering their environmental circumstances, the 36 percent of the respondents who answered affirmatively may have had reason to fear others.

Questions 61 and 62 probed for visual and auditory hallucinations, which are less susceptible to environmental factors. Hallucinations were experienced by fewer respondents than any of the other symptoms in the psychosis cluster. Thirteen percent of the respondents reported having visual hallucinations, and 17 percent reported auditory hallucinations. Hypnogogic hallucinations and hallucinations as sequelae of substance abuse may fall into this category. Almost one-third of the sample (31 percent) reported feeling as if they were "going crazy." Most of these (27 percent) felt that way "sometimes." Four questions were asked to determine orientation regarding time, place, and person. Results indicated that virtually all of the sample had clear orientation.

Thirty-five percent of the respondents said that they had a severe fear of diseases. This was the most frequently checked phobia. Again, this may be considered a realistic fear considering the circumstances of the homeless. After diseases, the most frequently checked phobic items were heights, guns, fires, knives, dying, and going crazy. The phobic items are listed in order of descending response frequency.

Table 7. Substance Abuse and Suicide, N = 158

Item Number	Mean	SD
Substance Abuse Items		
70. Do you drink heavily?	1.77	1.06
71. Do you take drugs?	1.34	0.66
Suicide Items		
82. Do you feel so sad that you want to kill yourself? (ideation)	1.26	0.49
84. Have you ever tried to kill yourself? (history of attempt)	27 yes response	(17 percent)
	131 no response	(82 percent)

1 = Never; 2 = Sometimes; 3 = Often; 4 = Always

Table 8. Psychosis Item Cluster, N = 158

Item Number		Never	Sometimes	Often	Always
57. Feel that you are	N	117	31	6	3
unreal	%	74	20	4	2
58. Things around you	N	95	50	7	6
seem unreal	%	60	32	4	4
59. People are trying to	N	100	48	8	1
harm you	%	64	30	5	1
60. Feel things are going	N	88	62	5	3
wrong in your body	%	56	39	3	2
61. See things that are not	N	137	16	4	1
there	%	87	10	3	0
62. Hear voices when no	N	131	21	2	2
one is there	%	83	13	2	2
63. Think you are going	N	108	43	5	2
crazy	%	69	27	3	1

On the organicity items, 21 respondents (15 percent) reported having seizures at times, and 34 respondents (21.5 percent) reported having blank spells (32 said sometimes, and two said always). Alcoholism and epilepsy should be considered when interpreting these responses.

CORRELATIONS BETWEEN THE ACL AND PSYCHOSOCIAL SURVEY

Pearson Product Moment Correlations were calculated for selected Adjective Checklist subscales and psychosocial survey cluster items. Seventy-eight correlations were calculated. Twenty-seven of these were significant at the .05 level. The small size of these 27 correlations (mean = 2077) suggests that a loss of variance has not been explained. Therefore, although they are statistically significant, the correlations may lack meaningfulness in terms of the actual relationship between the PSS and ACL variables which were examined.

There was a significant positive correlation between the aggression subscale on the ACL and the aggression–frustration symptom cluster on the PSS. The subjects who scored high on the aggression subscale thus also scored high on the aggression–frustration items. There was also a significant correlation between history of violent trauma as reported on the psychosocial survey and a high number of unfavorable adjectives checked on the Adjective Checklist. There was a negative correlation between the number of favorable adjectives checked on the ACL and depression item on the PSS. Thus, respondents who had high scores on depression described themselves with fewer favorable adjectives than those who did not score high on depression. Conversely, respondents who scored high on depression described themselves with significantly more unfavorable adjectives. Again, all of these correlations were low, explaining less than five percent of the variance, and the results must be interpreted accordingly.

DISCUSSION

Several characteristics of this homeless sample warrant discussion. This sample was comprised of a significant proportion of women and minorities. The group was relatively young and generally in touch with reality. Gross psychopathology was not prevalent despite a high rate of psychological trauma. A conscious effort to include women in the sample was made by interviewing subjects in homeless shelters for women. Our interviewers found that women, particularly those in the street, were less likely to participate in the study. We feel that homeless women probably feel more vulnerable and avoid contact with others in order to protect themselves.

A high percentage of our sample (70 percent) belonged to minority groups. It is well documented that unemployment, a housing shortage and other socioeconomic factors affect blacks much more critically than the majority population, particularly among the younger generation. Most of our subjects were relatively young, which concurs with other homeless studies finding a younger population among today's homeless.

It is important to note that a majority of our subjects had been homeless for less than three years. They were indeed the "new homeless." Our subjects were not new to New York City; a majority had been in New York for more than 11 years and had lost their residences as a result of financial difficulties. Often fire, condemned housing or extensive hospitalization had resulted in a loss of housing. Thus socioeconomic factors again played a key role in homelessness.

Another important point is that almost half of this sample had a high school education or better and approximately 30 percent had been employed in skilled technical occupations. These facts must be examined in order to comprehend the factors involved in homelessness.

Although a majority (88 percent) had living relatives, only 57 percent had contact with their relatives. The authors speculate that the decline in support systems within the family structure may account for the lack of contact with relatives. A majority (68 percent) of the subjects had friends, but only a proportion of this majority felt that they had someone to whom they could turn for help. Interestingly enough, subjects who participated in our study often referred other homeless persons on the street to us. There was clearly a homeless network in operation. The subjects were most often clean and well dressed and did not fit the homeless stereotype of the past. Almost one-fourth of the subjects were victims of child abuse, and almost one-half of these were victims of abuse which was sexual in nature. There is disagreement concerning the extent of child abuse; its occurrence is more frequent than reported according to the experts who attended the Third National Conference on Sexual Victimization of Children in Arlington, Virginia, in April, 1985.

In our sample, three times as many homeless women, compared to homeless men, had been victims of rape. The actual number of women who had been raped represented almost 38 percent of the entire sample of homeless women—a very high percentage. More than one-third of the sample feared being attacked in the shelter and on the street. Clearly our homeless subjects often felt at the mercy of their environment.

The most prominent clinical features for this sample were feelings of sadness and depression. A very high incidence of prior suicide attempts was also reported. Certainly the extraordinary stresses and perils of being without a home contributed to these expressions of despair. Feeling frustrated, irritable and annoyed by others were also reported with greater frequency than other items. These behaviors might be indicative of a difficult personality style or they might be logical responses to the chronic stress of intractable poverty and the social stigma of being homeless. Since we had no information on subjects' personalities before becoming homeless, it is impossible to gauge the role of homelessness in the etiology of clinical symptoms.

Almost one-half of the sample reported drinking heavily sometimes, often, or always. The drinking question was subjective; that is, each respondent defined "heavy drinking," as well as the frequency categories (never, sometimes, often, always), in his own way. A high incidence of alcoholism was reported anecdotally by the examiners, which corroborates the survey findings.

Alcoholism, physical illness, malnutrition, and the harshness of day-to-day life must be considered in interpreting the homeless person's responses to questions probing for psychosis. Forty percent of the sample reported that things around them seemed unreal at times.

Homelessness was relatively new for a majority of the sample, who may still have been surprised that they had fallen into such a state. Living on the streets may have seemed bizarre and unreal— feelings which under the circumstances do not indicate psychosis. This sample impressed the examiners as being generally intact psychologically with adequate judgment and the ability to relate to others. The survey indicated that the subjects definitely had clear orientation, with only 13 percent reporting visual or auditory hallucinations.

Considering the extraordinary trauma that these people sustained, it is not surprising that depression emerged as the most prevalent clinical feature on the psychosocial survey. Little correlation was found between responses on selected psychosocial survey items and selected Adjective Checklist subscale results. However, the subscale "number of unfavorable adjectives checked" and PSS depression items were positively correlated.

The extremely high incidence of physical trauma and the

frequent reports of depressive symptoms, anxiety, suspiciousness, and fearfulness suggest that post-traumatic stress disorder (PTSD) may be a significant problem for the nonpsychotic homeless. Future research is needed to determine whether or not homeless persons who have suffered severe trauma re-experience the traumatic events. Recurrent intrusive recollections and dreams of the event are significant symptoms of PTSD which were not investigated by this study.

Clinically, the sample was much more intact psychologically than those identified as former mental patients, who make up a significant segment of the homeless population. The clinical features our subjects reported indicate that they experienced a lot of psychic pain, but they were not out of touch with reality. The responses on both measures used in this study, particularly the Adjective Checklist responses, were quite variable. The fact that these homeless subjects chose to describe themselves in very different ways corroborates the heterogeneity of the "new homeless."

In conclusion, although there obviously is a segment of the homeless population which is not identifiably mentally ill, the high incidence of psychological trauma and other factors reported in this study indicate a need for some mental health intervention and treatment. As other investigations have recommended, both public and private agencies must develop strategies, policies, and treatment mechanisms and provisions for the homeless, including the "new homeless."

References

1. Gundy P: Money available to aid nation's homeless. JAMA 251:6, 1984

2. Pear R: Homeless in U.S., put at 250,000, far less than previous estimates. New York Times, May 2, 1984

3. Hopper K, Baxter E, Cox S, et al: One Year Later: The Homeless Poor in New York City. New York Community Service Society, 1982

4. Goodwin M: Koch and estimate board clash on renovating shelters. New York Times, April 13, 1984

5. English B: Homeless families on rise here. New York Daily News, April 22, 1984

6. Goleman D: Lawsuits try to force care for the mentally ill. New York Times, April 24, 1984

7. Lipton F, Sabatini A, Katz S: Down and out in the city: the homeless mentally ill. Hosp Community Psychiatry 34:817–821, 1983

8. Hoffman S, Nigro J, Rosenfeld R: Who Are the Homeless? New York, New York State Office of Mental Health, May 1982

9. Bahr H, Houts K: Can You Trust A Homeless Man? A Comparison of Official Records and Interview Responses by Bowery Men. Public Opinion Quarterly, 35:375–382, 1971

10. Bassuk EL: The homeless problem. Scientific American 251:40–45, 1984

5

A Mental Health Treatment Program for the Homeless Mentally Ill in the Los Angeles Skid Row Area

Rodger K. Farr, M.D.

5

A Mental Health Treatment Program for the Homeless Mentally Ill in the Los Angeles Skid Row Area

Recently a great deal of media attention has focused on the increasing number of homeless people in America. The problem has received much publicity, but very little has been done to try to understand the causes of homelessness or to devise ways to help this suffering segment of our population. The phenomenon of homelessness in America is not limited to the decaying areas of our large cities, but is a nationwide problem of grave national importance.

Until recently, most people thought the homeless "skid row" residents, or street people, were men and women who were either chronic alcoholics, derelicts, or dropouts from society who simply did not desire to better themselves. They were seen by our society as people who deviated so far from the American work ethic as to be not worth helping; however, this is not the case (1).

THE LOS ANGELES SKID ROW AREA

The Los Angeles Skid Row area covers approximately two square miles in the heart of downtown metropolitan Los Angeles. With a perimeter formed by freeways and the Los Angeles River, its boundaries are more psychological than physical. Rundown businesses, cockroach-infested hotels, railroad tracks, bridges, and numerous bars and liquor stores characterize its landscape. Although there are many private missions and shelters offering thousands of free meals a day and 1,800 free beds a night for those lucky enough to obtain them, most of the thousands of homeless residents end up sleeping in abandoned buildings, alleyways, garbage bins, under bridges, and so forth.

THE LOS ANGELES SKID ROW POPULATION

The population of the Los Angeles Skid Row area has changed markedly over the last 15 years. Previously it had been populated primarily by older men with a high proportion of chronic alcohol or drug abuse problems. In recent years, it has been invaded by large numbers of young chronically mentally ill men and women.

Deinstitutionalization

This change in population parallels the deinstitutionalization of the state mental hospital system in the United States over the past 20 years. We found significant numbers of homeless people in the Skid Row area who had previously been hospitalized in a mental hospital, as other investigators are now finding (2). Our work indicates that a large percentage (approximately 30 to 50 percent) of the hardcore homeless population of Skid Row are chronically and seriously mentally ill (3). They are not the winos or derelicts of the past but are often men and women from middle-class families who have experienced chronic mental illness and because of their mental disability, have been unable to make it on their own. They have trouble providing themselves with the basic necessities of life, such as food, shelter, and clothing.

For the purposes of this study, our definition of a homeless person is someone who spends a significant part of each year without shelter. Some of the homeless Skid Row residents receive County General Relief, which is about $228 per month, but more often than not, they find themselves on the street when their money runs out before the end of the month. Many homeless are unable or unwilling to apply for public assistance.

Demographics of Skid Row Homeless

The Skid Row population varies in number depending upon the time of year and the weather. We estimate that there are seven to 15 thousand homeless people inhabiting the area. During the winter months the number of homeless in Los Angeles can double. Because of cold weather in other parts of the country, the homeless migrate to Southern California. The street people refer to these migrating winter residents as "sun birds."

The recent recession aggravated, but did not cause, the homeless problem. When we began our work in January 1981, there were already an estimated 7,000 to 10,000 homeless people in the Skid Row area, and the recession of 1982 had not yet hit. According to the staff of the missions in Skid Row, the number of homeless mentally ill had been increasing during the 10 years prior to 1981, apparently in direct proportion to the closing of the state mental hospitals.

Our work in the Skid Row area in 1981 indicated that the Skid Row population contained approximately 80 to 85 percent men, 10 percent women, and five to 10 percent children. Women and children were seldom seen in the Skid Row area 15 years ago, but their numbers have risen rapidly in recent years, and there are now an estimated 1,000 women. The Skid Row male population is approximately 50 to 60 percent black, 20 percent hispanic, 20 percent white, and 5 percent American Indian, and the female population is 60 to 70 percent white, 20 percent black, and 15 to 20 percent hispanic.

What is significant is that almost 50 percent of the homeless Skid Row population suffer from some chronic, incapacitating mental illness. Our work shows that 30 to 40 percent of the male population of Skid Row suffer from a serious mental illness, while approximately 80 percent of the female homeless population suffers from a serious mental disability. A large number of those who are chronically mentally ill are overtly psychotic. We estimate that 75 percent of the psychotically mentally ill suffer from schizophrenia. Other recent studies across the nation have shown significant numbers of mentally ill among their homeless populations (4–6). We are currently completing an "Epidemiologic Research Study of the Homeless Mentally Ill in Skid Row," funded by the National Institute of Mental Health, and will soon have more definitive information concerning this population.

Acceptance Attracts Them to Skid Row

One of the main attractions of Skid Row to the chronically mentally ill is that they feel accepted there. Unfortunately, there are other attractions as well, such as alcohol, drugs, and violence. As a result, many of the mentally ill become involved with drugs, alcohol, or become victims of violence, all of which gravely aggravate their mental illness. Our work indicates that 40 percent of the mentally ill male population of Skid Row have a serious alcohol or drug problem, while only 15 to 20 percent of the female population have a serious alcohol or drug problem.

Greyhound Therapy

Many of the mentally ill homeless display behavior so bizarre as to make them socially unacceptable in the communities from which they come. In Skid Row, on the other hand, their behavior is tolerated. Many have spent time in mental institutions before coming to Skid Row. It is thus not uncommon to find persons who have been given "one-way bus tickets" out of their communities. "Greyhound Therapy" is one method some communities are using to deal with their chronically mentally ill (7). The Los Angeles Metropolitan Bus Terminal lies in the heart of Skid Row, and when mentally ill people arrive by bus, they simply lack the ability or coping stamina to get out of Skid Row.

THE PROBLEMS OF THE HOMELESS MENTALLY ILL

Destitute, Desperate, and Without Families

The majority of the homeless mentally ill are destitute. They are without adequate food or shelter and literally eat garbage and sleep in the streets. They are usually without family ties and have poor job histories. They are easily victimized by unscrupulous merchants and marauding gangs of hoodlums. Rape, assault, robbery, and even murder are commonplace daily events in Skid Row. The homeless have learned to be especially cautious on the days of the month when the General Relief or SSI disability checks are due, when roving gangs of hoodlums come to prey. The dangers of living in the Skid Row area are enormous, but for many, the dangers seem to be outweighed by the degree of freedom they experience and the tolerance for their abnormal behavior.

Inability to Utilize Traditional Services

The homeless chronically mentally ill are unable to utilize many of the traditional social support services because of the nature of their chronic mental illness, their fear of government agencies, and the inaccessibility of the programs.

Fear of Government

They are so frightened of authority figures that some seldom venture out of the Skid Row area, even to seek food or medical care. For many, prior contacts with authority figures and mental health professionals have led to imprisonment or institutionalization. They do not trust the system, some with good reason.

Independent Nature

Many of the homeless mentally ill are unable to live in a structured community environment. Their mental illness keeps them from enjoying the human contact and companionship which they so desperately need, and their independent nature also isolates them. Many cannot handle money properly and may give it away.

Medical Problems

Their inability to seek medical care, combined with the physically unsanitary manner in which they live, frequently leads to serious health problems. The medical problems we have seen in the homeless mentally ill population are at times devastating and are more characteristic of the populations of underdeveloped countries than of America.

Rejection of the Mental Health System

Periodically many of the homeless mentally ill will spend time in an acute psychiatric hospital. They are hospitalized only when their behavior becomes so unacceptable that the police are forced to pick them up. We found that the vast majority would rather live in filth and be subjected to beatings and violence than to be institutionalized, even in our finest mental hospitals. This is a stunning indictment of our mental health treatment system and is indicative of our inability to understand or to help this segment of the mentally ill population.

Lack of Services

We found a lack of government health and social support services in the Skid Row area. The main government presence is represented by the Department of Public Social Services (DPSS) and the police. There are few health facilities in the area, and before the development of the Skid Row Project, the nearest mental health facility was five miles away.

The Children of Skid Row

In recent years, an increasing number of undocumented, Spanish-speaking women and children have migrated into Skid

Row. Many are in the United States illegally and therefore are unable to utilize traditional social, medical, and mental health treatment systems. Many are undocumented Hispanic women who work for extremely low wages in the garment industry located in the Skid Row area. In a recent survey, approximately 1,200 children were found living in Skid Row, with an estimated 80 to 90 percent being undocumented hispanic children and 70 percent under the age of eight. These children suffer from a different set of mental health problems than the homeless adults. Their mental health problems are frequently the result of "cultural shock," sexual molestation, child abuse, and exposure to the very real physical dangers in Skid Row. The children of Skid Row, like the adults, are trapped there and lack the ability or resources to leave.

THE DEVELOPMENT OF THE SKID ROW MENTAL HEALTH PROJECT

DPSS Personnel Problem

The homeless mentally ill problem in the Los Angeles Skid Row area came to light somewhat by accident in January 1981 (3). A request for help from the County DPSS triggered an investigation that eventually led to the establishment of the Skid Row Project. DPSS had been experiencing serious personnel problems with their staff in the Civic Center District Office (Skid Row). These problems finally culminated with the stabbing death of a much loved DPSS worker in December 1980. As a result of a request for help, in January 1981 the author was sent by the Department of Mental Health to assist the DPSS workers in Skid Row and to assess the mental health problems present there.

Grave Mental Health Problems

It was apparent that the mental health problems that existed in Skid Row were grave and of a far greater magnitude than had previously been suspected. Increasing numbers of DPSS workers were becoming frightened, frustrated, and intimidated because of the overwhelming number of seriously mentally ill people they were seeing. There was a grave need to establish a permanent mental health service in the area, but because of severe financial cutbacks in funding to the Department of Mental Health, it was apparent that there would not be significant resources available for developing a new community mental health center in Skid Row. The situation was desperate, however, and some type of mental health assistance had to be developed.

The Beginning of the Project

By the spring of 1981, the Skid Row Mental Health Project had been organized, and a number of ongoing mental health programs were in operation. A weekly mental health consultation clinic was arranged for the DPSS staff, enabling them to review cases with a mental health professional and to review their own reactions to their mentally ill clients. Eventually the consultation clinic was available on a daily basis with a mental health professional stationed in the DPSS office. Regular mental health educational seminars were arranged to give the DPSS staff a better understanding of the mental illnesses they were seeing in their clients and to assist them in dealing more effectively with these clients. These programs significantly helped to reduce the stress and frustration of the DPSS staff, tensions decreased, and disagreements became less common. The very presence of a mental health professional on a regular daily basis in the DPSS office served as an important factor in quieting some of the fears and concerns of the DPSS staff.

Mental Health Problems Were Widespread

As the work progressed, it became clear that a large portion of the population of Skid Row was suffering from severe mental illness and was unable to reach out for help because they lacked the ability to engage the existing social, health, and mental health systems.

By July 1981, a full-time mental health professional was added to manage the day-to-day operations of the Project. The staff of the early Skid Row Project was comprised of the author (on a part-time basis), a small number of student and volunteer mental health professionals, and a very dedicated DPSS social worker. The Project, initially housed in the DPSS office, was born out of a team effort between DPSS and the Department of Mental Health. This team effort, which continues today, is absolutely vital in order to address the multifaceted problems of the homeless mentally ill, who urgently require social services, including food and shelter and mental health services.

Project Grew in Size

By the fall of 1981, an additional full-time psychiatrist had been added to the Project. By the winter of 1981/82, mental health outreach and consultation programs to many of the missions and shelters in Skid Row had been added. By the fall of 1983, the Project had grown to a staff of eight mental health professionals with clerical support staff, and offered a wide variety of innovative mental health programs, including extensive outreach and community consulting programs and a daily 8:30-to-5:00 mental health treatment clinic, which was located in a large Skid Row shelter.

GOALS OF THE SKID ROW PROJECT

Early Goals

One of the early goals of the Project was to survey and evaluate the community resources available within the Skid Row area. This survey revealed that there were numerous private missions, agencies, and self-help groups operating in the Skid Row area. Together, these organizations offered a formidable amount of resources and assistance to the homeless Skid Row residents. These private agencies traditionally had grown out of religious or community groups that had formed missions in response to the cries of the helpless and wretched. Although these missions addressed the physical (food and shelter) and spiritual needs of the inhabitants of Skid Row, their staffs had little or no mental health training or understanding, and in recent years they had felt overwhelmed by the increasing number of mentally ill residents. The Project established regular mental health consultation services to the staffs of these missions and agencies.

Mental Health Patch

The Project provided a "mental health patch" for the existing programs of the missions and agencies in Skid Row, consisting of mental health consultation, education, emergency crisis intervention, and a system of referral linkages.

Mission Staff Provides Unique Care

It was found that the staff members of many of the missions were eventually able to provide a unique treatment service that professional mental health workers could not provide. Many of the staff members of the Skid Row missions were "graduates of the streets" and thus were accepted and trusted by the Skid Row residents, including the homeless mentally ill. Because of the unique treatment service offered by the mission staff, the professional mental health staff of the Project were given a rare opportunity to reach an otherwise untrusting and unreachable population. This unique partnership has been essential in the work of the Project.

The Development of Concerned Agencies of Metropolitan Los Angeles (CAMLA)

Early in our work with the missions and agencies in Skid Row, we noted an interesting problem—although many of the missions had been operating for 30 years or more within a few blocks of each other, there had been very little ongoing communication among them. They were able to recognize the fragmentation of services and lack of coordination and communication, and we assisted them in the development of a community organization, a "coalition" of agencies, missions, and people working together. This organization is called "CAMLA" (Concerned Agencies of Metropolitan Los Angeles). The formation of CAMLA in early 1981 served as a spark to unite the various organizations in Skid Row into what has become a true community support network. CAMLA has subsequently grown into a viable, well-structured organization with a membership of over 55 different agencies and groups. In 1983, CAMLA was incorporated as a private, nonprofit corporation and has an office in a major shelter building. CAMLA is expanding its goals to include transportation services and information and referral and will continue to act as a common voice for the Skid Row community. Although the early development of CAMLA was heavily influenced by the Department of Mental Health, it rapidly assumed a life and direction of its own and now stands as an independent community organization. Greater understanding between governmental and private agencies in Skid Row, resulting from the development of CAMLA, has markedly improved and increased utilization of services by the homeless.

The Skid Row Directory

Recognizing the need for a directory of services and resources available in the Skid Row area, the Department of Mental Health together with CAMLA developed and prepared a 100-page *Directory of Services in the Skid Row Area*. The Directory was prepared in a binder, permitting constant updating and revisions as new resources and agencies were added. It listed each of the private and public agencies, the services that they provided in the Skid Row area, and the name of a key contact person within each agency. It was cross-indexed alphabetically and by type of service offered. Four hundred directories were printed and distributed. The cost of printing was covered by a private donation by a local organization. A small, eight-page pocket version of the Skid Row Directory, which lists vital services and resources and includes directions for easy use, was prepared by the Department of Mental Health and

CAMLA. We hope to have 15,000 copies printed and distributed to the residents of Skid Row. An interesting side benefit was a strengthening of the bonds and relationships among the agencies and organizations that worked together to prepare the directory.

Direct Treatment Service Added

Early goals of the Skid Row Project were to provide mental health consultation, education, emergency crisis management, and evaluation and referral. In addition, some direct treatment services were provided, and these direct services have been greatly expanded in the past two years. They are primarily geared to crisis handling, mental health evaluation, individual and group therapy, medication management, vocational rehabilitation, and mental health evaluations to establish eligibility for various disability programs, such as the federal Social Security Disability Program.

The SSI Clinic

Significant numbers of homeless mentally ill persons are mentally disabled and are eligible for assistance under the Social Security Disability Program, but they do not apply. Many are so severely mentally dysfunctional that they would meet even the most stringent criteria for eligibility under the current Social Security disability guidelines. Paradoxically, however, because of their severe mental symptoms, they are unable to follow the very difficult bureaucratic procedures necessary to gain access to the Social Security Disability Program. The Project established a daily "SSI Clinic" to assist mentally disabled homeless persons in gaining access to the federal SSI Disability Program. Strategies and procedures were developed to provide these persons with appropriate psychiatric evaluations. In order to assist these persons through the long and arduous SSI application and appeals process, it is necessary to assume a kindly and supportive advocacy role. The Project works closely with several community legal advocacy groups on the SSI program. The success rate of persons accepted into the SSI Clinic Program has been greatly increased by the SSI Clinic.

Fiscally, the SSI Clinic has proven to be quite sound. Mentally disabled persons who receive Los Angeles County General Relief support are paid an average of $228 per month. We estimate that for every 400 persons who are converted from General Relief to SSI support, Los Angeles County saves over $1 million in tax revenues each year. This does not include the additional savings to the county resulting from the fewer DPSS personnel that are needed to manage the General Relief Program once these people are removed from the General Relief role. Once these people are accepted into the SSI Program, they receive approximately $425 per month (that is almost double the General Relief support) and are then eligible for a variety of medical and mental health treatment programs under state and federal coverage. Providing assistance in entering the SSI Disability Program has become, in and of itself, an important and significant mental health treatment process for the homeless mentally disabled. The SSI Program appears to be one of the few long-range assistance programs for the mentally disabled.

Treatment Programs Must Be Innovative and Responsive

Traditional mental health treatment approaches usually are not effective in reaching or treating homeless mentally ill persons. A mental health treatment program for the homeless mentally ill should include some stabilization of their immediate physical environment, the provision of shelter, food, and physical health care, and protection from violence—all significant aspects of the mental health treatment process. It is very difficult to help these people without first establishing rapport and trust. We were able to establish the necessary trust through our close relationships and linkages with the existing Skid Row missions and agencies. It is necessary to deliver the type of mental health care that these persons can accept and in a location where they will accept it. Often this means establishing and delivering mental health services in missions and agencies. Some of the outreach and mental health programs that the Project has developed are unique and somewhat unorthodox. Some of our most successful programs have been "piggy-backed" or "patched" onto existing programs in missions and agencies.

Drop-In Rap Sessions

Ongoing weekly group therapy programs were conducted in the missions. The term group therapy, in the traditional sense, does not apply to these groups. We refer to them as "drop-in rap sessions." There were no formal requirements for participants as any attempt to force them to follow traditional bureaucratic procedures, especially the securing of their last name, could frighten them. Pressing bureaucratic requirements and regulations on them only resulted in their leaving the program. Mental health professionals must learn to live with this type of loose arrangement and limited goal setting in order to be of assistance to this unique group. The goals of the weekly "rap sessions" were to help the members understand their mental illness and mental health treatment methods and approaches and then to link them with existing mental health treatment programs. Another goal of the rap sessions was to instruct members on how to survive in Skid Row.

The Need for a Sense of Belonging

One rap session for women was held in a day care center for homeless women. This center was founded and run by a compassionate woman who was a former DPSS worker who had noted the increasing number of destitute women in Skid Row. This center, located in what was once a dilapidated storefront, has operated for over six years and is run entirely on private donations. It assists up to 500 women per year, but many must be turned away because of the large number of women in Skid Row. Unfortunately, the center is open only during the day and does not offer beds for the women. It does provide them with a vital sense of belonging and caring—something they have rarely experienced because of their life styles and their chronic mental problems. The women cook their meals together, celebrate birthdays and holidays together, and find a safe refuge in the center from the frightening and hostile world they see outside. This sense of belonging and sharing offers a unique mental health treatment to these women. The goal of the Skid Row Project was to provide a mental health "patch" to the center's existing mental health program. In later years, the center was able to develop professional mental health treatment services privately on its own.

Mental Health Facilitator

The physical presence of the Skid Row Project has in itself been of great value as a sign of support and concern to the residents and agencies of Skid Row. The Project has acted as a "mental health facilitator" and has served as a vital missing link between these agencies and the mental health treatment system.

Rapid Transit District (RTD) Clinic

The lack of low-cost transportation in the Skid Row area has been a major problem to the residents, hindering their attempts to secure employment, housing, medical care, and vocational rehabilitation. The Skid Row Project developed the "RTD Clinic" (Rapid Transit District) to assist Skid Row residents in obtaining special low-cost RTD bus passes. The RTD pass is easily obtained by completing a simple form that certifies that one is transportationally disabled. Then a bus pass can be obtained for $4 per month, whereas a regular pass costs about $30 per month—a sum which is beyond the reach of many Ski Row residents. With the RTD pass, one can travel anywhere within the greater Los Angeles area.

The pass has thus become a passport for the residents and an important mental health treatment tool. It enables them to escape from the hell of Skid Row and seek employment, housing, medical care, and other previously unobtainable opportunities. Many of the residents were willing to accept medical care from a private medical facility but would not accept care from a government medical facility. In an attempt to make medical care available to the Skid Row residents, the Skid Row Project developed a liaison with a primary care center in a local private hospital. Skid Row residents could then travel to the front door of this primary care center using their RTD passes.

Work Projects and Vocational Rehabilitation

Another serious problem among the homeless mentally ill is the lack of availability of vocational rehabilitation or employment counseling. The Skid Row Project has been working with the Los Angeles County DPSS to develop work projects for the homeless mentally ill. We found that under a little-used county regulation, persons who receive General Relief assistance from the county must be given an opportunity for employment through county work projects at various county facilities, such as gardens, offices, parks, and recreation areas. There are over 100 locations available, and we feel that these work projects will serve as an extremely valuable vocational rehabilitation tool. Work, even on a very limited basis, will raise the self-esteem and confidence of the homeless. We are also working with private and state vocational rehabilitation agencies to develop transitional work therapy projects for Skid Row inhabitants. Vocational rehabilitation and work, however limited in scope, are vital long-range goals for any permanent resolution of the homeless cycle.

The Police in Skid Row

When we first began our work, we noted that there was a lack of understanding and relationship between the police and many of the agencies serving the Skid Row area. The Skid Row Project, together with CAMLA, has developed an excellent working relationship with the police. A police department representative is a member of CAMLA and has participated in the "rap sessions." As a result of this cooperation, we have found that the police now have a better understanding of the mental health problems of residents and do a much better job of handling them. The severely mentally ill can and must be directed into mental health treatment programs, not incarcerated in jails.

Revolving Door Syndrome

A continuing problem noted among the mentally ill in Skid Row is the "revolving door syndrome." The syndrome is not unique to the homeless mentally ill, but is common to all the chronically mentally ill. It is characterized by multiple short periods of psychiatric hospitalization with little follow-up or continuity of care between these periods. The Project is attempting to develop a community support system base for the homeless mentally ill as an alternative to costly repeated hospitalizations. We believe a stabilization center in the Skid Row area could provide support, companionship, and caring during a short period of intensive mental health treatment. An ideal stabilization center should provide a period of five to seven days of living in the center in which the homeless mentally ill not only would receive intensive mental health care but also would be "cleaned up, rested up," and given appropriate medical care, social services, vocational evaluation, and linked with the various public and private agencies that would give the additional vital care and support needed for a more long-range resolution of their problems. We envision the stabilization center as a joint public sector–private sector endeavor, operating out of one of the shelters. The price of such a stabilization center and community support program would be paid for many times over by the savings through decreased utilization of psychiatric hospitalization, emergency-room care, jail detention, and the like.

Self-Help Groups

We are in the process of developing a Skid Row chapter of a local self-help group for the mentally ill. Self-help groups can offer the long-range support and caring vital to the recovery of the chronically mentally ill. The chapters existing outside Skid Row would offer a bridge once a person was ready to move.

Recent Expansion of Service

The program has grown enormously over the last four years, currently has a staff of 24, and occupies 4,250 square feet of space located in a homeless shelter in the middle of the Skid Row area with an annual budget of approximately $800,000. It offers a wide variety of mental health treatment programs now helping hundreds of the homeless mentally ill. Some of these treatment programs include:

1. Outreach and early identification of the homeless mentally ill in Skid Row
2. Regular mental health consultation to homeless shelter and agency staffs
3. Psychiatric evaluation for SSI and other disability programs
4. Advocacy and assistance for homeless mentally ill to gain access to health and social services programs
5. Group therapy and "drop-in rap sessions"
6. Crisis evaluation and management
7. Outpatient treatment
8. Medication treatment and monitoring
9. Day-care program
10. Psychosocialization programs
11. Vocational program
12. Self-help and support group meetings
13. Case management
14. Money management (in association with the Social Security Administration)
15. Seven-day-a-week drop-in center, available to anyone who needs help
16. Certification of individuals for low-cost transportation passes (RTD clinic)
17. Priority programs targeted especially for homeless women, children, and those who are the most vulnerable
18. Facilitating and advocacy for the homeless mentally ill
19. Assisting patients into placement in long-range care and residential facilities when appropriate

20. Triage to acute psychiatric hospitalization when necessary
21. Operation of joint programs with drug and alcohol rehabilitative agencies

Private Business Involvement

The Skid Row Project has encouraged the involvement of the private sector. For example, a large donut chain daily donates to the Project a large quantity of fresh donuts, which serve as a valuable aid in attracting hungry persons off the streets to become initially involved in the Project programs. The Project has negotiated with a large aerospace firm to donate the services of alcohol and drug abuse counselors on a regular basis.

Cost of the Project

The overall cost of the Skid Row Project has been low, considering the results of the program and the numbers served. The cost for the Project was initially defrayed, in part, by the fact that the office space used by the Project was often provided free of cost by the missions and agencies it served. These agencies felt that the mental health support and services they received more than compensated them for the free office space they provided. The initial office equipment and furniture used by the Project was salvaged from discarded county furniture or provided through charitable gifts. The offices were initially refurbished and painted by Department of Mental Health employees who volunteered their services after working hours. The use of "volunteer professional staff" is encouraged and the experience has proven valuable to the volunteer professionals. We currently have social work interns, psychology interns, and psychiatric residents from the local universities working at the Project.

PROGRAMMATIC GOALS IN PLANNING FOR THE HOMELESS MENTALLY ILL

Los Angeles County has recently been named the "Homeless

Capital of the United States." The result of a study released in the spring of 1984 by the U.S. Department of Housing and Urban Development (HUD) estimates that there are between 30,000 and 35,000 homeless people in Los Angeles County. Although most of the attention has been focused on the homeless mentally ill in Skid Row, the situation is a county-wide one. The Skid Row area contains the largest single concentration of the homeless, an average of 10 thousand, but there are at least 11 other areas of concentrated groupings of the homeless in Los Angeles County (8). In addition, there is a diffuse infiltration of homeless persons throughout the entire county. They tend to seek out areas such as isolated neighborhoods and small shopping centers where there is less chance of being harmed, and the pickings of food in the garbage cans is better.

Some of the homeless mentally ill in Los Angeles are very mobile and tend to wander from one area to another—from outlying areas into Skid Row and back again. Any systematic or effective approach to help this population as a whole must be on a county-wide or regional basis in order to have any significant or lasting effect. It is vital to remember that long-range solutions must be included in any planning approach. In the past, the mental health treatment programs for the homeless mentally ill have been more of a "bandaid" type of approach, with few long-range solutions. The dollars and other resources spent over the lifetime of these persons to "put out fires" is wasted and does little to bring about any resolution to the problem or to provide long-range help or stability for them.

As outlined in "A Programmatic View of the Homeless Mentally Ill," (8) two basic approaches should be considered in planning for mental health care for the homeless mentally ill: the target groups approach and the phased intervention approach.

The Target Groups Approach

Given the present limited resources of the public mental health treatment system and the large numbers of homeless mentally ill, consideration must be given to selecting target groups from within the general homeless population. It is very difficult to be selective, because all of those suffering deserve the opportunity to receive help. However, with current resources so limited and the need so great, if one does not single out target groups, one can soon become overwhelmed, and no one will receive any assistance.

Selection of specific target groups should be made with several principles in mind: which groups are more acutely at risk, which groups are more amenable to treatment, and which groups offer the best long-range opportunity for salvageability.

With this in mind, the following "target groups" may be considered:

1. *The newly arrived, homeless mentally ill.* Our work in the Project has shown that the longer a chronically mentally ill person remains homeless, the more difficult he is to reach and the more resistant he becomes to mental health treatment. At times, the newly arrived mentally ill homeless are still taking antipsychotic medication or have just recently discontinued the medication. They are more in touch with reality, and treatment rapport is more easily established with them. Some still have some fragment of a relationship with their family or previous mental health treatment program. It is important to capitalize on these remnants of family relationships. At times, contact with the family can be re-established, and with guidance and support, it may be possible to return these persons to their home communities and their families. The Skid Row Project has an excellent working relationship with various agencies who provide free transportation back home.

   The newly arrived are also less likely to have been subjected to the alcohol, street drugs, or the violence so prevalent in Skid Row. These facts severely aggravate underlying mental illness and make help much more difficult to provide.

2. *Battered and at-risk children and runaway youths.* Children and runaway youths are generally much more amenable to treatment and are more salvageable. There are excellent examples of what can be done with innovative and nontraditional treatment approaches to at-risk and battered homeless children,

much as the "Para Los Ninos" Program in Skid Row. The Project has several mental health workers assisting this excellent private agency.

3. *Homeless women.* There is a significantly high incidence of mental illness among the homeless women of Skid Row (we found approximately 80 percent). They lack the basic self-defense skills necessary for survival of most homeless men and are frequently victims of violence. They are very vulnerable and should be targeted early for outreach and assistance.

4. *Homeless elderly.* This group is most vulnerable and defenseless, and should receive high priority for assistance.

Phased Intervention Approach

In general, traditional mental health treatment approaches do not work for the homeless mentally ill; that is why they are homeless. In planning mental health treatment programs for this population, one must be creative, innovative, and compassionate and assume an advocacy role. Outreach is an essential ingredient to any program that assists this group.

It is helpful to think of mental health treatment or intervention for the homeless mentally ill in three basic phases when considering the development of programs:

Phase 1, the emergency first-aid phase. This phase is somewhat equivalent to a "batallion aid station" in a battle zone. In this phase of intervention, emergency assistance is given under acute circumstances. Programmatic goals are early identification and outreach, emergency mental health consultation, training for shelter and other agency personnel, and the "patching" of a mental health program onto existing shelter and agency programs. Development of mental health "drop-in centers" in large catchment areas of the homeless can provide a temporary "safe haven" and a focal point from which first phase intervention goals and objectives can be accomplished.

Phase 2, the stabilization phase. During the stabilization phase, the homeless mentally ill receive an opportunity to spend anywhere from five to seven days in a "stabilization center." This center should be set up in cooperation with a private shelter or agency that is known and accepted by the homeless mentally ill. At the center they would be given an opportunity to clean up, rest up, and get physical health care as well as intensive mental health care. They would also be provided with linkages to other services, such as social services, vocational rehabilitation, counseling, and so forth. It is anticipated that as many as one-third of the homeless mentally ill could be stabilized in this center to return back to their families, communities, and other appropriate mental health care facilities and programs.

Phase 3, the long-range solutions phase. Long-range solutions to the problems of the homeless mentally ill must be found if any of the programmatic planning is to have lasting benefits. It is of very little value to give shelter and intensive emergency mental health treatment to a person unless this is followed up by some long-range solution to the problem. The "stabilization phase" should automatically be followed by long-range programs for those who require continued long-range mental health care. The Social Security Disability Program, vocational rehabilitation, Veterans' Administration benefits, board-and-care facilities, and so forth, should all be a part of the long-range treatment program. Placement in a therapeutic living center may be necessary for those who are unable to cope with life on their own or do not have a family or supportive structure to return to.

SUMMARY

The plight of the homeless mentally ill has received considerable media attention in recent years, but little of any substantive nature has been done to alleviate their suffering. They are seen in ever increasing numbers in communities across the nation, and their very presence is a testimony to the failure of our society and its mental health treatment system. They have become a grave problem of national proportions and implications. "The streets have become the asylums of the 1980s" (9) for many of the chronically mentally ill in America.

The homeless problem has become a political battleground in the last few years, and Los Angeles has received the dubious honor of being dubbed the "Homeless Capital of America." We have found in our work among the homeless in the Skid Row area of Los Angeles that between 30 to 50 percent suffer from some serious or incapacitating mental illness. Los Angeles has become a repository for many of the nation's homeless mentally ill in part because of its climate and its liberal social atmosphere and because other communities have used "Greyhound Therapy" (a one-way bus ticket out of town) to get rid of their chronically mentally ill.

The homeless mentally ill are generally without family ties, are defenseless, and are frequently victimized. They are beaten, robbed, and raped daily. They fall prey to many physical diseases because of their exposure to the elements, malnutrition, poor hygiene, and their inability to get basic medical care. They often eat garbage and sleep in alleys and under bushes. They are incapable of utilizing our traditional social, medical, and mental health care systems. In many ways, these systems were never designed to be accessible to the gravely mentally disabled, and fail one of the very populations that they should be serving.

The homeless mentally ill population is the product of many factors. The deinstitutionalization movement of the last 20 years discharged hundreds of thousands of state mental hospital patients into the community with little planning and support. New liberalized mental health laws made involuntary psychiatric treatment almost impossible. It was thought that the new psychiatric "wonder drugs," which were to be the panacea of the mentally ill, combined with the development of local community mental health centers would prevent the necessity of long-term psychiatric hospitalization. Unfortunately, the dollars never followed the patients, and only a fraction of the local community mental health centers were ever built. A system of community care and social support for the mentally ill was never developed.

Society, in general, has seemed unwilling to accept the chronically mentally ill back in the community. The result has been that many of the chronically mentally ill have not been able to cope with life on their own and have eventually become homeless, ending up on the streets of the skid rows of America. Some communities have attempted to deal with their chronically mentally ill by ignoring them or offering "Greyhound Therapy." The Los Angeles Skid Row area has become a dumping ground for thousands of these helpless, hopeless, chronically mentally ill persons. In a nation as rich and progressive as America, it is inconceivable that this type of problem is allowed to exist today.

The Los Angeles County Department of Mental Health Skid Row Project was developed to help this homeless chronically mentally ill population. The Skid Row Project has developed some unique and innovative treatment mechanisms and methods for reaching out to and helping this special population. Traditional mental health approaches have proven of little value to this population; it is essential to deliver the type of mental health care they can accept in a location where they will accept it. A "storefront approach" and a "patching" of mental health programs upon existing and accepted homeless shelter programs has proven very successful where traditional approaches have failed.

When we began viewing food, shelter, warm clothing, medical care, and a safe, caring environment as part of a mental health treatment program, we were finally able to provide meaningful help to this population. Programmatic planning approaches for the homeless mentally ill should include intervention phases and targeted population groups. Outreach, early identification, and an advocacy approach are also essential. We found that commonsense treatment approaches, such as "rap sessions" in the shelters, "SSI Clinics," and "RTD Clinics" were readily accepted. It must be remembered that the homeless mentally ill problem is a multifaceted one that requires multifaceted approaches. A team approach between the public and private sectors is essential. The Skid Row Project provided a leadership role in assisting public and private agencies to more appropriately address the needs of the homeless in Skid Row through the development of a community coalition named CAMLA.

In 1982, the Skid Row Project was given the National Association of Counties (NACO) Achievement Award as one of the most innovative mental health programs in the nation. The project has served an important role in helping to alert Los Angeles County and other communities across the nation as to the seriousness and magnitude of the problems of the homeless mentally ill.

This project demonstrates that community mental health can assume creative, innovative, and nontraditional roles. Caring, reaching out, and a team approach are essential if one is to meet the special needs of the homeless mentally ill. It is hoped that the Skid Row Project can serve as a working model for other communities that are attempting to help this destitute and suffering population.

REFERENCES

1. Baxter E, Hopper K: Private Lives, Public Spaces: Homeless Adults on the Streets of New York City. New York, Community Service Society of New York, 1981

2. Appleby F, Desai P: Documenting the relationship between homeless and psychiatric hospitalization. Hosp Community Psychiatry 36:732–745, July 1985

3. Farr R: The Los Angeles skid row mental health project. The Journal of Psychosocial Rehabilitation 8:64–76, 1984

4. Arce A, Tadlock M, Vergare MJ, et al: A psychiatric profile of street people admitted to an emergency shelter. Hosp Community Psychiatry 34:812–817, 1983

5. Lipton F, Sabatini A, Katz S: Down and out in the city: the homeless mentally ill. Hosp Community Psychiatry 34:817–21, 1983

6. National Institute of Alcohol, Mental Health, and Drug Abuse: The ADAMHA Round Table on the Homeless: a report on the round table on homelessness in America held by the National Institute of Alcohol, Mental Health, and Drug Abuse. Rockville, MD, 1983

7. Farr R: Street People: Is This The Plight of Our Chronically Mentally Ill? Overholser Memorial Day Presentation Paper. Washington DC, St. Elizabeths Hospital, April 1984

8. Farr R: A programmatic view of the homeless mentally ill in Los Angeles. International Journal of Family Psychiatry (in press)

9. Farr R: Testimony from hearings before the U.S. House of Representatives, District of Columbia Subcommittee. Congressional Quarterly, March 19, 1985

6

Organizational Barriers to Serving the Mentally Ill Homeless

Joseph P. Morrissey, Ph.D.
Kostas Gounis, M.A.
Susan Barrow, Ph.D.
Elmer L. Struening, Ph.D.
Steven E. Katz, M.D.

6

Organizational Barriers to Serving the Mentally Ill Homeless

Before the dramatic increases in the homeless population became an issue of public concern, observers of skid rows and other marginal urban areas noted the growing presence of psychiatrically disabled persons among the ranks of the homeless. New York City's Bowery area, for example, was described in the mid-1970s as "a psychiatric dumping ground," and in Berkeley, at around the same time, former psychiatric patients were becoming a visible element within the population of street people (1–3). However, it has only been during the 1980s that homelessness entered public consciousness as a crisis of major proportions and the mentally ill in the streets, shelters, parks, and transportation depots have become the focus of controversy.

Debate about the homeless mentally ill has centered on two issues: who has been responsible for creating the problem, and what should be done to solve it? These issues have been argued about in various guises. The issue of responsibility, for example, has been defined in terms of the proportion of homeless people who are mentally ill. That is, the prevalence of mental illness among the homeless is seen as an indicator of the role that mental health policies, such as deinstitutionalization, have played in the growth of homelessness, and of the extent to which mental health systems should bear the burden of providing solutions (4, 5). The numbers controversy reflects contrasting views of the causes of the increase in homelessness—in particular, the relative contribution of mental health policies versus socioeconomic changes, such as loss of low-income housing, social service cutbacks, unemployment, and general economic policies and trends (6, 7). A parallel argument concerns the extent to which the sources of homelessness lie in the homeless themselves: that is, do individuals "choose," whether on the basis of psychopathology or life-style preferences, to be homeless, or are they the victims of social and economic processes beyond their control (6, 8)?

Positions on these issues have frequently been sharply polarized, and in some locales, proponents of one or another view have argued their cases in courts of law, where decisions about the responsibility of various agencies have increasingly been made (9–11). Although this has done little to foster consensus, it has necessitated a shift away from questions of historical culpability and refocused the debate on the more concrete problems involved in defining and responding to the needs of people who are both homeless and psychiatrically disabled.

In fact, the most recent writings on the homeless mentally ill present a veneer of agreement on the following critical issues: namely, that substantial numbers of homeless people have severe and chronic psychiatric disorders; that neither basic subsistence nor clinical needs are currently being met; and that meaningful responses must address clinical issues in the context of meeting basic needs (12). Yet such generalities do not easily translate into programs of action. Moreover, the unresolved questions that informed the debate over the causes of and responsibility for homelessness among the mentally ill (psychopathology versus lack of housing; and the role of mental health systems and policies) resurface in the face of decisions about designing, staffing, administering, and funding residence and service programs for psychiatrically disabled homeless persons.

The trial and error approach to serving this population may be inevitable at this stage. But given the absence of established guidelines for meeting both housing and treatment needs, it becomes particularly important to describe and assess current programming efforts to address these needs in order to mitigate organizational barriers to service delivery and in order to enhance future planning efforts. We will focus on one such effort, undertaken by state, municipal, and voluntary agencies in New York City. The Creedmoor initiative, which this chapter describes, is of particular interest because, unlike some of the other innovative efforts to serve the homeless, it is directed exclusively at that portion of the population with serious psychiatric disabilities. The Creedmoor initiative is still in its formative stages and many of the specifics of program development remain to be worked out. But in contrast to most psychiatric services for homeless people, the Creedmoor programs will provide both emergency and longer-term housing as well as clinical services. The unique, or prototypical, aspects of the Creedmoor initiative thus deserve careful observation and assessment.

THE CREEDMOOR INITIATIVE

Although large public shelters can provide for basic needs, such as a bed and food, they are unable to provide for the psychosocial needs of the mentally ill homeless. Most shelters are not connected with clinical services and thus stand outside the network of psychiatric services within the community. The shelters themselves do not offer a full range of treatment and rehabilitation services, and there have been few options available to meet the specialized needs of their residents who are mentally ill (13).

In this context, the development of a specialized shelter for the mentally ill homeless with on-site mental health services and an adjacent long-term residence on the grounds of the Creedmoor Psychiatric Center in Queens, New York, represents an innovative approach to the problem. First opened in November 1983 as a generic, temporary shelter to meet the escalating demand for shelter space in New York City, the Queens Men's Shelter (QMS) was converted over the ensuing year to a 200-bed shelter for the mentally ill homeless with on-site mental health clinic services. In addition, as part of the New York State Office of Mental Health's Residential Care Center for Adults (RCCA) Program (a new alternative housing initiative for the mentally ill who require supervised living arrangements), an administratively separate, long-term residential unit with 196 beds was opened in January 1985 in the same building occupied by the QMS. Thus the Creedmoor program brings together under one roof a continuum of service components—temporary shelter, mental health services, and longer-term residence—which otherwise need to be negotiated and pieced together from separate community agencies, if the services are available at all.

The Creedmoor initiative involves a collaborative effort between the public and private sectors. The Shelter is operated by the New York City Human Resources Administration (HRA) in a former patient treatment building of the Creedmoor Psychiatric Center. HRA operates the city-wide shelter system and is the agency responsible for public welfare and income maintenance programs. HRA staff provides for daily maintenance of Shelter residents as well as social service and entitlement registration. In addition to the building, the New York State Office of Mental Health (OMH) provides funding for the operation of the on-site mental health clinic and for the start-up costs of the RCCA program, including the renovation of one wing of the building as a residential unit. OMH clinical staff working as outreach teams in the New York City shelter system also are involved in the identification and referral of clients to the Shelter. The voluntary sector is involved both through the operation of the clinic and RCCA as well as through the provision of services to RCCA residents. The clinic and RCCA are operated by Builders for Family and Youth, Inc., an affiliate of the Catholic Charities of Brooklyn. Residents of the RCCA will receive basic support services on site, but it is expected that they will utilize off-site services in the voluntary sector for their medical, psychiatric, rehabilitative, and vocational needs.

Although the start-up costs of the RCCA have been absorbed by the OMH, it is anticipated that RCCA will become largely self-supporting through the residents' payment for board and care from Supplemental Security Income (SSI) congregate Level II funding. This financing plan is consistent with the goals of the overall

RCCA program (which is targeted at a broader population than the mentally ill homeless) to provide long-term residential services at a cost less than current per-diem rates in state psychiatric centers.

The aim of the Queens Men's Shelter is to provide a relatively protected and stabilizing environment where, in the context of meeting the basic needs for food and a bed, mentally ill men drawn from the rest of the New York City shelters can be evaluated and treated for their psychiatric needs. Also, the Shelter program is intended as a transitional mechanism through which clients requiring supervised housing may be referred to community residences and other alternative housing arrangements.

The goals of the RCCA are to provide safe, humane housing for persons who are not in need of inpatient psychiatric care, yet who do require a supportive environment not presently found in the community. Although its residents will not be required to become actively involved in treatment programs, with the exception of minimum psychiatric and medical reviews as prescribed, staff of the RCCA will attempt to engage residents in activities that might eventually lead to participation in treatment or rehabilitation programs. Staff will also periodically assess residents for their potential to move to more independent living situations. When the program attains full occupancy with 196 residents, it is anticipated that the RCCA staff will total 54 positions, including administrative, support, rehabilitation, and case management personnel.

Our ongoing research and evaluation activities are focused on a holistic assessment of the Creedmoor initiative. One component examines the processes of case-finding and referral into the Shelter and RCCA, while the other addresses a more formal evaluation of the RCCA program. OMH Shelter Outreach Teams serve as case-finders within the New York City shelter system to identify appropriate homeless men for referral to the QMS. As the program operates on a voluntary basis (in other words, none of the Shelter or RCCA residents are "committed" or involuntarily admitted), a variety of self-selection processes inevitably occur between the points of case-finding, enrollment, and continuance in one of the program components. That is, all clients who are identified as candidates for the temporary Shelter may not accept a referral, and furthermore, not all of those who are referred to the Shelter will choose to remain there or to participate in the QMS's mental health clinic or in the RCCA. Many of those who are enrolled may also be referred to other mental health or residential programs after a brief stay, while others will continue as long-term residents of the "temporary" Shelter or RCCA.

We are gathering descriptive data at each stage of these selection processes so that client profiles can be constructed in order to compare those who are selected with those who are eliminated at the points of case-finding, referral, enrollment, and continuance in the Shelter and RCCA programs (14). Such information will enable us to determine which segments of the overall population of homeless mentally ill men are successfully engaged in each of the Creedmoor programs (Shelter, clinic, RCCA) and which segments refuse to participate or are screened out for other reasons. To the extent that the clients who are successfully engaged are unrepresentative of the larger population of homeless mentally ill men, program planners will have an empirical basis for estimating how much of the overall problem can be met with programs similar to Creedmoor, and how much will require other types of housing and service delivery initiatives.

With regard to the RCCA program, a two-stage evaluation plan has been developed. The first stage is largely descriptive, focusing on methods of data collection and analysis to obtain a profile of the characteristics and experiences of the initial cohort of RCCA clients. These procedures will allow for an early assessment of the extent to which the OMH's goals for the Creedmoor RCCA are being realized. Critical issues to be examined in this regard are the lag-time for full program occupancy, the actual cost-offsets relative to inpatient care, the residents' quality of life and use of services, and the rate of transition to other community housing alternatives. Once the program achieves operational stability, the second stage evaluation will begin to consider more enduring issues, such as the cost-effectiveness of the program and the kinds of homeless mentally ill persons for whom the program is most successful.

SOME GENERIC SERVICE DELIVERY ISSUES

Many of the service delivery issues encountered in the development and operation of the Creedmoor programs for the mentally ill homeless are generic organizational problems common to all efforts to intervene with this vulnerable and difficult-to-reach client population. We will highlight several of these issues and discuss potential barriers that warrant close examination and assessment by all program developers and evaluators involved in serving the mentally ill homeless.

The assumptions underlying this initiative must be carefully assessed. It is expected, first, that the Shelter will be a desirable destination for a significant portion of the mentally ill clients in the municipal shelter system; second, that the mental health clinic will successfully engage most, if not all, of the clients who are referred to the Shelter; third, that housing alternatives will be available in addition to the RCCA; and, finally, that the RCCA will be a desirable long-term housing arrangement for those who cannot make the transition to more independent living. For the goals of this program to be achieved, most clients will have to transition through each component of the program. The extent to which this program is successful in identifying, engaging, treating, and referring "appropriate" clients is largely dependent on the validity of these assumptions.

The mentally ill homeless, whether in the streets or in the shelters, constitute a highly visible reminder that "gaps" in the provision of comprehensive care and "cracks" in the service system do indeed exist (15, 16). All too frequently the expression "falling through the cracks" is used to describe the fate of this population (12). Any effort to address this problem may necessarily involve, as in the case of Creedmoor, the establishment of an interagency, multicomponent network to provide the means for sufficient client access, for comprehensiveness and continuity of care, and for appropriate selection. Therefore, we must examine the principles governing the selection process for engaging this population, the organizational framework which provides the flow of clients and resources, and the preconditions for ensuring continuity of care.

The Selection Process

The concept of *client selection* refers to the process through which the encounters between a client and a given organization or organizations result in definitions and decisions about which groups are suitable for and which actually become involved in the program. The selection process for engaging and serving the mentally ill homeless involves, as Creedmoor suggests, a number of stages in which different types of persons or organizations serve as agents of selection. When a program operates on a voluntary basis, particular attention must be paid to factors that shape self-selection—the client's decision whether or not to accept and then follow through on a referral. *Service refusal* is a function of where and how mental health services are being offered and how they are perceived by the client (17). To the degree that emphasis on structure and compliance takes priority over outreach and a nondemanding, "no-questions-asked" approach, certain types of potential clients are likely to refuse services or drop out (18, 19).

A significant factor that shapes these encounters is the differing perceptions of need and the appropriate responses to needs between service providers and potential clients. We may encounter clients that have been selected for a program who are utilizing the services for different purposes than those intended by the providers (19). The marginal social existence of the homeless, including the homeless mentally ill, often means that services and resources are "reinterpreted" and used for more fundamental needs. An emergency room may thus serve as a refuge during a cold night; a hospital admission may be sought as a temporary respite from the precariousness of life in the streets; a mental health clinic may become more significant as a source of coffee and subway tokens than as a treatment program; the security of a bed in a specialized "psychiatric" shelter may count for more than the services being offered. Service providers often use the term "therapy bums" to describe this phenomenon of "service abuse." Although "abuse" undoubtedly takes place, our concern should be to understand patterns of use by allowing for the possibility of differing perceptions of needs.

Organizational Framework

On another level, *organizational selection* may develop a tendency to define the targeted groups in accordance with explicit or implicit professional and organizational goals and limitations. The problem of "creaming" or "skimming" (20, 21) the target population to fit the program, rather than developing a program to fit the target population, inevitably becomes the issue *par excellence* in these encounters. The challenge of the mentally ill homeless for urban psychiatry is the difficulty in *finding* them, the difficulty in *engaging* them, and the difficulty in *serving* them. It is widely recognized that the mentally ill homeless fall into multiple groupings and that there are significant differences among street people, public versus private shelter users, and those who avail themselves of other residential units (22). Street people are less accessible to treatment interventions because they are harder to find and respond more often to less demanding outreach programs than to traditional more highly structured mental health services. Thus, the "treated" population inevitably becomes the tip of the iceberg—only a selected subset of the overall population.

The issue of selection becomes even more critical when the process involves *interorganizational* integration. In the case of Creedmoor, the multicomponent network that is considered necessary for ensuring continuity of care requires a considerable degree of interorganizational coordination. Selection practices at this level inevitably constitute an important set of influences in shaping the process of referral, admission, and engagement of the client. The different agencies involved may exercise different degrees of "boundary control," meaning that some segments of the population targeted by one agency may be deemed unsuitable for the services by another (23). The different persons and agencies making the referrals and the decisions regarding eligibility cannot always be expected to apply the same criteria throughout the entire process. A significant number of potential clients are likely to get "lost" in the bureaucratic maze involved in locating, evaluating, and admitting a person into the program—in the case of Creedmoor, from a municipal shelter to the QMS to the mental health clinic.

We have tried to show that the clients who are eventually engaged by the program are the outcome of selection mechanisms operating at various levels and at different points during the process. Another aspect that warrants careful examination is the set of conditions deemed appropriate, or even necessary, in order to ensure comprehensiveness and continuity of care. The Creedmoor initiative suggests that the concept of a specialized, "psychiatric" shelter, even when it is intended as a much needed "asylum" for such a vulnerable and needy group as the mentally ill homeless, poses a central dilemma. A specialized shelter is based on the principle of separating the mentally ill from the rest of the shelter population so that a select group can be created to sustain a service intervention program. Separation, however, in the eyes of many of those concerned, becomes segregation and exclusion rather than the first step in a process of reintegration into community living. The history of the asylum in America provides a poignant example of this dilemma (24).

Ensuring Continuity of Care

We have already encountered numerous indications of the difficulties that the Creedmoor program will have in attracting the targeted group of mentally ill men from the municipal shelter system. Initially, its location on the grounds of a state psychiatric facility was a deterrent to those potential residents who prefer to stay away from the mental health system. The isolation and remoteness of the program from the inner city where the homeless, including the homeless mentally ill, have established various "niches" inevitably contribute to the unwillingness of the homeless men to be transported elsewhere. Inner city areas offer greater tolerance, perhaps, and the availability of more street-level resources and places to spend the day. Community resistance, a well-known phenomenon in residential neighborhoods with regard to congregate housing for the mentally ill and other dependent populations, also influences potential shelter-users, who want to avoid yet another source of harassment, and referral agencies, who want to avoid further alienation of local community groups (25–27). Such opposition has already been a prominent part of the local community reaction to the Queens Men's Shelter (28, 29).

These issues will affect the nature of Creedmoor's clientele and thus the scope of the program's role in addressing the problem of the homeless mentally ill. The impact of the Creedmoor initiative will also reflect the more generic consequences of the effort to provide comprehensiveness and continuity of care. To the extent that the accumulation of former psychiatric patients within the homeless population is seen as a failure of mental health systems to assure continuity of services, continuity of care can be seen as an essential ingredient of a responsive and responsible service system (13, 17). However, the ideal of client movement along a continuum of coordinated services addressing different levels of need may be difficult to achieve outside of a relatively self-contained, quasi-institutional system. The trade-off here is that the effort to narrow the "gaps" or "cracks" can result in limiting services to a narrow segment within the homeless population—those who will be least resistant to moving from the relatively unrestrictive environment of the streets or shelters to a more institutional setting.

Finally, we believe that the innovativeness of Creedmoor and similar programs should not be seen as an attempt to provide a wholesale solution to the clinical and housing needs of the homeless mentally ill. Instead, we must be prepared to learn from the impact of the Creedmoor initiative—by looking at which needs of the mentally ill homeless are appropriately met as well as at the limitations and difficulties that the program will encounter. We have already noted that we will be examining the characteristics of the clients who are successfully engaged by this program in an effort to determine which segments of the mentally ill homeless population they reflect. Underlying this concern is our belief that the homeless mentally ill, and the homeless in general, do not constitute a homogeneous population in a way that makes one specific type of program the one most appropriate solution to their needs. This recognition obviously underlies the RCCA's rationale in that the program is designed for those mentally ill homeless who require supervised living arrangements. But even this definition is not specific enough. As the program unfolds, ambiguities will be encountered. The way that such ambiguities are resolved will determine the relative success of the Creedmoor initiative and our ability to draw the appropriate lessons from it.

The Creedmoor initiative is only one of several innovative efforts being undertaken by public and private agencies around the country. Ultimately, it will be necessary to move beyond the assessment of individual programs to look at the relative effectiveness of a variety of services, including drop-in centers, missions, outreach programs, emergency shelters (both with and without on-site clinical programming), and a continuum of housing options which entail varying degrees of structure and supervision. Moreover, as Bachrach and others have pointed out, model programs that may be highly successful with a selected subgroup of clients often lack generalizability to the group as a whole and the potential impact of the program on the larger problem is thus limited (30). Thus, any effort to assess the Creedmoor initiative requires attention to competing or complementary service models and to the broader population of psychiatrically disabled homeless who may be little affected by such models.

References

1. Reich R, Siegel L: The emergence of the Bowery as a psychiatric dumping ground. Psychiatr Q 50:191–201, 1978

2. Segal S, Baumohl J, Johnson E: Falling through the cracks: mental disorder and social margin in a young vagrant population. Social Problems 24:387–400, 1977

3. Segal S, Baumohl LJ: Engaging the disengaged: proposals on madness and vagrancy. Social Work 25:358–356, 1980

4. Bassuk E: The homelessness problem. Scientific American 251:40–45, 1984

5. Lipton S, Sabatini A, Katz S: Down and out in the city: the homeless mentally ill. Hosp Community Psychiatry 34:817–821, 1983

6. Hopper K, Hamburg J: The making of America's homeless: from skid row to new poor, 1945–1984. New York, Community Services Society of New York, 1984

7. New York State Department of Social Services: Homelessness in New York State: A Report to the Governor and Legislature. Albany, NY, 1984

8. Drake R, Adler D: Shelter in not enough: clinical work with the homeless mentally ill, in The Homeless Mentally Ill. Edited by Lamb HR. Washington DC, American Psychiatric Association, 1984

9. Baxter, E, Hopper K: Shelter and housing for the homeless mentally ill, in The Homeless Mentally Ill. Edited by Lamb HR. Washington DC, American Psychiatric Association, 1984

10. Goleman D: Law suits try to force care for the mentally ill. New York Times, April 24, 1984

11. Margolick D: Ex-mental patients upheld on suing. New York Times, March 28, 1984

12. Talbott J, Lamb HR: Summary and recommendations, in The Homeless Mentally Ill. Edited by Lamb HR. Washington DC, American Psychiatric Association, 1984

13. Bachrach L: The homeless mentally ill and mental health services: an analytical review of the literature, in The Homeless Mentally Ill. Edited by Lamb HR. Washington DC, American Psychiatric Association, 1984

14. Morrissey J, Tessler R: Selection process in state mental hospitalization, in Research in Social Problems and Public Policy, vol. 2. Edited by Lewis M. Greenwich CT, JAI Press, 1982

15. Bachrach L: Continuity of care for chronic mental patients: a conceptual analysis. Am J Psychiatry 138:1449–1456, 1981

16. Morrissey J, Goldman H: Cycles of reform in the care of the chronically mentally ill. Hosp Community Psychiatry 35:785–793, 1984

17. Goldfinger SM, Chafetz L: Developing a better service delivery system for the homeless mentally ill, in The Homeless Mentally Ill. Edited by Lamb HR. Washington DC, American Psychiatric Association, 1984

18. Lamb HR: Deinstitutionalization and the homeless mentally ill. Hosp Community Psychiatry 35:899–907, 1984

19. Wiseman JP: Stations of the Lost. Englewood Cliffs, NJ, Prentice Hall, 1970

20. Kirk S, Greenley J: Denying or delivering services? Social Work 19:439–447, 1974

21. Nagi S: The organizational context of evaluation: when norms of validity fail to guide gatekeeping decisions in service organizations, in Evaluation and Accountability in Human Service Programs. Edited by Sze W, Hopps JC. Cambridge, MA, Schenkman, 1974

22. Barrow S, Lovell A, Struening J: Evaluation of programs for the mentally ill homeless: progress report. New York City, Community Support System Evaluation Program, New York State Psychiatric Institute, 1984

23. Greenley W, Kirk S: Organizational influences on access to health care. Soc Sci Med 10:317–322, 1976

24. Morrissey J, Goldman H, Klerman L: The Enduring Asylum. New York, Grune and Stratton, 1980

25. Baker B, Seltzer B, Seltzer M: As Close As Possible: A Study of Community Residences for Retarded Adults. Boston, Little, Brown, 1974

26. Baron R, Piasecki J: The community versus community care, in Issues in Community Residential Care. Edited by Budson R. San Francisco, Jossey-Bass, 1981

27. Segal S, Aviram U: The Mentally Ill in Community-Based Shelter Care. New York, John Wiley, 1978

28. Leahy J: Renew demand to shut shelter. New York Daily News, March 7, 1984

29. Ain S: Protesters hit Creedmoor. New York Daily News, April 2, 1984

30. Bachrach L: Overview: model programs for chronic mental patients. Am J Psychiatry 137:1023–1031, 1980

7

Summary

Steven E. Katz, M.D.

7

Summary

The noteworthy advance in the study of the mentally ill homeless in these chapters is the result of moving our research endeavors out of the institutions into the shelters and onto the streets. This is an important development since accurate data about this growing social tragedy will be available only when the phenomenon of homelessness is studies "in vivo."

In the United States, the total number of homeless persons remained virtually constant from the time of the Great Depression until 1979. The population was predominantly composed of the stereotypical skid row "bowery bum." When the number of homeless persons began to increase, the population was initially swelled by the addition of deinstitutionalized mentally ill persons who had been released from state psychiatric facilities in the 1970s. As the subsequent evolution of homelessness has unfolded, the following facts have emerged:

1. The total number of homeless persons is significant and rising steadily, fueled by social, economic, and political factors. Current estimates range from 250,000 to 3,000,000 persons nationally.
2. The composition of the homeless population is changing. The average age is now placed in the late 20s to middle 30s; there are

increasing numbers of women, families, children, adolescents and minorities.
3. The relative percentage of mentally ill in the total homeless population has decreased from 60 to 80 percent in 1980 to 25 to 35 percent in 1985.
4. Drug abuse (25 to 35 percent) and alcoholism (30 to 40 percent) are rampant.
5. Incidences of transient and situational homelessness have increased dramatically (in other words, persons have lost their jobs, apartments, or homes but do not see themselves as chronically homeless).

In New York State, it is estimated that there are 49,000 homeless persons, including families, of which 7,300 require mental health services. In addition, another 4,200 persons are de facto homeless, because they currently reside in state psychiatric centers and have no home of record. In New York City, as many as 7,000 homeless persons and 2,800 homeless families are housed nightly with the demand for these services continuing to increase. With respect to the need for mental health services, the screening of over 30,000 people in New York City's homeless shelters revealed that between 25 and 33 percent have either a history of psychiatric hospitalization or evidence of serious mental illness. Of that group, two to three percent required hospitalization, and another seven percent, emergency outpatient intervention.

A review of the chapters in this monograph demonstrates clearly that we have become increasingly sophisticated in our methodological approaches to the understanding and treatment of the homeless mentally ill.

Dr. Levine and Mr. Stockdill provide extensive review of the plight of the homeless in Chapter 1. They indicate the need for public and private agencies to address the problem of the homeless and provide specific recommendations on the homeless issue. The comparative study of the shelter populations served in 1982 and 1983 in Philadelphia, discussed by Drs. Vergare and Arce in Chapter 2, demonstrates findings that support the basic trends described by Dr. Jones and his colleagues in Chapter 4. These trends are as follows: a significant decrease in chronic homelessness (43 percent to 10 percent), increased episodic and situational homelessness, more prevalent histories of treatment for mental illness and most significant, the efficacy of an appropriate range of services, including a walk-in service, extended evaluation, shelter, and extended housing for the psychiatrically impaired homeless.

Creative, aggressive treatment programs are a necessity with this population. A successful program must be based on an integrated biopsychosocial treatment plan which is specific in its knowledge of the demographic, economic, psychosocial, and medical status of the persons treated. A community-based residence with an on-site multidisciplinary team was utilized with emphasis on a highly individualized approach that addressed the entire spectrum of needs. The crucial factors in the success of the program appear to be multidisciplinary staff, the multifocal approach, and effective linkages to hospitals and community-based agencies. This group of homeless men was found to be heterogeneous in its psychosocial make-up and to exhibit mental, physical and social illnesses; they needed residential, financial, medical, psychiatric, and social supports. The early results of this multifocal, multidisciplinary approach have been promising. Its long-term efficacy and cost effectiveness are yet to be established.

In Chapter 4, Drs. Jones and Goldstein, and Ms. Gray, have provided data that support empirical observations that the homeless population is becoming increasingly young, minority (70 percent), and sexually balanced (41 percent women). The evidence substantiates the increasingly transient and changing nature of the homeless population. Fifty-three percent of the sample studied had lived in a home one year earlier and over 90 percent of the group reported previous employment. The increased specificity in defining personality types and character traits of the homeless, compared with the broad diagnostic categories utilized in earlier studies, is an advance in understanding the evolution of homelessness and perhaps will be helpful in making predictions about who will be at risk in the future.

The initiatives undertaken in Los Angeles, presented by Dr. Farr, in Chapter 5, are noteworthy because of the sponsorship of a private/public consortium. Nontraditional, innovative approaches to the problems of the homeless mentally ill were instituted. The initiative relied on minimal tax dollars at a time when public funding was becoming less available. Dr. Levine and Dr. Stockdill's comprehensive description in Chapter 1 of the federal government's efforts by the Departments of Health and Human Services and Housing and Urban Development and the anthology of public/private sector responses illustrates broad-based acknowledgment of the enormity of the problem of homelessness and the diversity and scope of responses to it.

Therapeutic intervention for the mentally ill homeless in New York includes mental health shelter teams and mobile outreach teams which provide psychiatric evaluation and treatment in the shelters, on the streets, and in the community. In addition, the Queens Men's Shelter and its companion, 196-bed residential care center for adults (RCCA) have been established on the grounds of the Creedmoor Psychiatric Center, Queens, New York. Dr. Morrissey and his colleagues discuss the Creedmoor initiative in Chapter 6. Creedmoor was designed to serve the short-term shelter and extended therapeutic residential needs of the homeless mentally ill. Mental health services are provided on site and in the surrounding community under the auspices of Catholic Charities of Brooklyn, a voluntary agency. The mental health services include screening, clinic treatment, continuing treatment, day treatment, crisis intervention, outreach, case management, and short-term rehabilitation. Preliminary results reveal remarkably high attendance rates for clinic appointments and unusually high compliance with medication schedules. Persons are referred for admission to the congregate care facility by Office of Mental Health teams that deliver mental health services to the homeless in shelters.

In New York, Residential Care Centers for Adults (RCCA) are designed to provide humane congregate care, therapeutic living environments, and psychiatric services for 80 to 200 mentally ill persons. In addition to the Queens Men's Shelter, 600 more residential care beds are planned for during the coming year under the auspices of both voluntary agencies and state workers. The centers are conceptualized as extended care facilities in which persons can remain indefinitely, if necessary. Active treatment programs will be provided on site with a continuum of services emphasizing rehabilitation. Residential care centers will be utilized extensively, but not exclusively, for the homeless mentally ill and, in addition, approximately one-half of new community residence beds in New York State will be earmarked for the same population.

This monograph presents ample evidence that we are moving into a more mature phase in both our understanding of the history of the homeless mentally ill and the development of innovative treatment approaches. New findings have emerged which must be considered in approaching the population and developing effective programs. These persons are chronically mentally ill, exhibit recurrent episodes of decompensation, abuse drugs and alcohol, and have minimal to nonexistent social support systems. They tend to be fiercely independent and resist relinquishing their freedom, even if appears to be in their own best interests. Therefore, programs must be aggressive in attempts to "recruit" patients, treatment plans must be developed on an individualized basis at the earliest moment of the patient's contact with the system, and mental health workers must be prepared to change the plan whenever it is clinically indicated. The plan should allow the greatest possible freedom, encourage the patient to handle his own finances, provide a living environment that is as unrestrictive as possible, encourage treatment for alcohol and drug problems, utilize crisis intervention and case management, and offer substitute social support systems.

Homelessness is the national social tragedy of the 1980s; all levels of government and the private sector must unite to develop comprehensive approaches if meaningful progress is to be made. The answers will not come easily, but the problem must be addressed.